John Hus and the Czech Reform

JOHN HUS

and the

CZECH REFORM

By

Matthew Spinka

ARCHON BOOKS

HAMDEN, CONNECTICUT

1966

LIBRARY OF CONGRESS CATALOG CARD NUMBER: 66-18645
PRINTED IN THE UNITED STATES OF AMERICA

Dedicated to

THE PEOPLE OF JOHN HUS

"I trust God that . . . the rule of thine affairs shall again be restored to thee, O Czech people!"

TABLE OF CONTENTS

INTRODUCTION

THIS monograph is strictly limited in scope. Its sole theme is Hus's alleged Wyclifism, for it was chiefly this charge on which he was tried and condemned by the Council of Constance. Was it true? That it was is too often the untested assumption, even of otherwise reputable modern historians. To ascertain the truth or falsity of this presupposition, to subject the notion to a critical examination, are the aims of this study.

Beyond the objective thus delimited this modest work does not aspire or venture. Accordingly, it makes no pretense of exhaustiveness, nor does it deal with questions outside these limits. But in the pursuit of this aim the author has utilized most of the literature bearing on the subject, both source materials and secondary works, particularly as far as the modern Czech research in this field is concerned. However, he has not had access to unpublished sources. Consequently, it is with a keen awareness of the tentative character of this little work that he offers it to the scholars in this field with the hope that it might prove helpful and useful. If it presents no new material, it at least gathers together the best contemporaneous thought on the subject, offering particularly the conclusions of Czech scholarship which otherwise might remain inaccessible.

For the aid received by him from outstanding Czech historians—Dr. F. M. Bartoš and Dr. Otakar Odložilík—the author is duly grateful, and hereby acknowledges his indebtedness to them. He also wishes to express his sincere thanks to his colleague, Professor John T. McNeill, for reading the work in manuscript and proof, and for many valuable suggestions.

MATTHEW SPINKA

1

I

WAS HUS AN INDEPENDENT THINKER?

I

THE figure of John Hus towers high among all those whom the Bohemian people have contributed to the roll of world's choice spirits. Historians throughout the passing centuries since the death of Hus have generally expressed high admiration of the heroic qualities of his character, the purity of his life, the clarity of his thought, and the zeal of his reforming purpose. He was the best product of the native reform movement, and the chief inspiration of those later religious groups which became the glory of the Czech nation. Some historians would go as far as to count him among the earliest of Protestant Reformers, or at least, to use the phrase of Ullmann, a Reformer before the Reformation. It is not too much to say, then, that John Hus—along with the Unity of Brethren—is the chief contribution of the Czech Reformation to the religious history of Western Christianity.

Hus was held in devoted reverence by the leaders of the Reformation, particularly by Martin Luther. The German Reformer published three letters of Hus and the protest of the Czech and Moravian nobles to the Council of Constance,[1] and enthusiastically recommended his writings to his followers. In a preface to the official *Confession of Faith* prepared by the Unity of Brethren and submitted in 1535 to him for approval (but not published until in 1538), Luther testified that the reading of the works of Hus had had a considerable influence on his conversion:

For indeed, while I was yet a papist, I was for long a most fervent emulator of the Roman traditions. (The papists of our times who write against us, are not as serious as I was, but are wholly cold, and are motivated either by hatred or by the desire of profit; they would do the same against the papists,

[1] *Epistolae quedam piisimae et eruditissimae Johannis Hus . . . Addita est D. Martini Lutheri praefatio* (Vitembergae MDXXXII); in D. Martin Luthers *Werke* (Weimar, 1914), L, 23-34.

if they could expect from us greater profit or glory.) But while I was a papist, I hated the Picard Brethren sincerely and from my heart, out of a great zeal for God and religion, and not on account of desire of lucre or glory. For, when by chance I came upon some books of John Hus, and found them to be powerful, and in accordance with the pure Word of God, I began to feel terrified why the pope and the Council had burned such and so great a man. Terror-stricken, I closed the book, fearing that with the honey there might lurk poison by which my simplicity might be infected. So violently had the name of the pope and the Council fascinated me!

But when it pleased Him who had separated me from my mother's womb to reveal to me that son of perdition . . . searching out all whom the pope had condemned and put to death as heretics, I praised them as saints and martyrs.[2]

Moreover, the father of Protestant historical research, Matthias Flacius Illyricus, himself a Slav, was likewise a sincere admirer of the Czech Reformer; he issued for the first time in Nürnberg in 1558 two folio volumes[3] containing almost all the Latin works of Hus and his Czech *Postil*. He thus made available the works of Hus long before the writings of Wyclif were made easily accessible. Accordingly, the former's chief works have been known since the middle of the sixteenth century, while the publication of Wyclif's writings was not undertaken until late in the nineteenth century.

This circumstance offers a partial explanation of the fact that prior to the nineteenth century it was through the mediation of Hus that the thought of Wyclif was chiefly known. The influence which Hus has thus exerted is due in some degree to a historical accident of the prior publication of his works, as well as to the forceful and effective presentation of the ideas. Consequently, it is not Hus's fault that he has received credit for much which in reality had been propounded by Wyclif, from whom Hus had derived it. Nevertheless, his dependence upon the English Reformer has always been freely conceded, though without prejudice to the priority of the native influence. Augustus Neander, who made a thorough study of the writings of Matthew of Janov,[4] one of the predecessors of Hus in the native movement of church and moral reform, concluded that Hus was

[2] "Vorrede zu *Confessio fidei ac religionis baronum ac nobilium regni Bohemiae*, 1538," in *Werke* (Weimar, 1914), L, 379-380.
[3] *Joannis Hus, et Hieronymi Pragensis confessorum Christi Historia et Monumenta* (Noribergae . . . MDLVIII).

grounded primarily in the thought of the native movement, and only in a secondary fashion had derived his inspiration from Wyclif. Neander went so far as to say: "We find in the principles of Janov the incipient germ of the whole reform movement in Bohemia, and it might have remained wholly national, wholly independent of the English spirit."[5] Although this had been written before the writings of Wyclif become available in published form, modern Czech scholars on the whole agree with Neander's judgment as against those who would make Wyclif almost the sole source of Hus's doctrinal views.

It may be affirmed, then, at the outset that Hus was the product of the native reform movement. The ever-deepening knowledge of this phase of Czech religious history assures Hus a secure place and an influential rôle in the movement. Beginning with Conrad Waldhauser, an Augustinian monk who had come to Prague in 1363, and the apocalyptic mystic, John Milíč of Kroměříž, whose fervent reform activity had begun in 1363 when he had resigned all his honors and began his passionate denunciation of the clerical and lay corruption, the early Czech Reformation may be said to have culminated in the work of Hus and his party. The most important theological exponent of the earlier native movement before the days of Hus was Matthew of Janov (d. 1394), the learned master of arts of the University of Paris. He had studied theology for six years, although without receiving a degree in divinity.[6] Denouncing vigorously and untiringly the moral depravity of the clergy, the excessive reverence paid to images, saints, and relics, he advocated as the means of reformation a daily participation in communion through which the believer was to be brought into fellowship with God. He was tried in the archiepiscopal court and forbidden to preach. Instead, he engaged in an assiduous literary activity, which resulted in the preparation of his extensive *Regulae veteris et novi testamenti*. In it, Matthew incorporated Milíč's treatises

---

[4] Matthew's chief work, *Regulae veteris et novi testamenti*, was published in five volumes (I-IV, Inspruck, 1908-1913; V, Praha, 1926).
[5] Augustus Neander, *General History of the Christian Religion and Church* (Boston, 1854), V, 270.
[6] Vl. Kybal, *M. Matěj z Janova* (Praha, 1905).

about the Antichrist, and William de St. Amore's *De periculis novissimorum temporum,* which had been declared heretical by Pope Alexander IV. Hus continued the tradition of his predecessors, despite the fact that Wyclif's literary influence upon him was considerable.[7] In the opinion of Václav Novotný, one of the chief modern authorities on *Husitica,* Hus often lightened the drudgery attendant upon literary composition by adopting Wyclif's verbal form, even when the intrinsic thought was his own or was derived by him from the native tradition.[8] The chief characteristic of the Czech reform was its emphasis upon preaching in the vernacular, and moral reform of the clergy and the people—not theological speculation or anti-ecclesiastical revolt. It may be affirmed—although at the risk of over-simplification— that Czechs were more interested in moral and ethical conduct, pure life, than they were in doctrine. For even the most advanced proponents of this movement did not side with the contemporary theological radicalism which advocated—it is interesting to note—such measures as the observance of the Sabbath instead of Sunday, the denial of the necessity of the baptism of children, and the assertion of the rightfulness of the baptism of adult believers at the age of thirty.[9] Rather, the leaders trusted in preaching, in transforming the springs of human action. Accordingly, at the Bethlehem Chapel, founded in 1391 for the purpose of furthering the aims of the reform movement, preaching was accounted the chief function of its clergy. It was stipulated that two preaching services be conducted every Sunday and holiday. And it was in the pulpit of this chapel that Hus exercised his greatest influence as the leader of the reform movement. It is unthinkable that Hus would have been called as its preacher, to succeed a famous member of the reform party and his own teacher, Stephen of Kolín, had he not been looked upon even then, at the beginning of his career, as an outstanding advocate of the program of moral reform. For he was called to

[7] V. Novotný, *Náboženské hnutí české ve 14. a 15. století* (Praha, n. d.), 212-13, 215.
[8] V. Novotný, *M. Jan Hus, jeho život a učení* (Praha, 1919-21), I, 71.
[9] L. Šimek, ed., *Jakoubka ze Stříbra, Výklad na Zjevení sv. Jana* (Praha, 1932), I, 37, 526.

that leading pulpit only a year after his ordination to the priesthood (1402), at the age of thirty-three. In fact, the conscientious and earnest young university professor must have been considered as a remarkably gifted preacher, as well as possessed of unusual reformatory zeal, to be chosen for such a responsible post. But he had a message, and like Paul he felt that "woe is me if I preach not!" Moreover, had he not been in the forefront of the native reform movement, and fully in sympathy with it, the recognition he had won for himself would be exceedingly difficult to account for.

Since a great many sermons, covering practically his whole active ministry, are extant, it is possible to estimate fairly correctly this phase of Hus's activity. Practically all his sermons are textual, replete with allegorical interpretation, and abounding in quotations from the Scriptures and the great Fathers. From the modern point of view, many would perhaps be pronounced dull and tedious; they appear to be a running commentary upon the text, rather than sermons constructed upon the accepted homiletical principles of our day. The allegorical exuberance of his imagination sometimes strikes the modern reader as fantastic: for instance, he explains the text, "and He entered a village," to mean that Jesus entered the womb of Mary, i.e., was incarnated.[10] Nevertheless, many of the sermons are moving and eloquent. The preacher consistently aims at reformation of morals. Moreover, the reader feels, and the hearer must have felt it much more powerfully, that there is no humbug or sham about the preacher of Bethlehem. His words ring true because his life is pure. Strongly ascetical in his emphasis upon the work of sanctification, he denounces unsparingly, and with almost monotonous reiteration, all carnality, such as the sexual irregularities of the clergy and the monks, avarice, money-grubbing, gluttony, drunkenness, rich apparel, pride, dice-playing, dancing, hunting, and simony. His ideal is distinctly other-worldly; he stresses world-forsaking, self-disciplining, humble life of voluntary poverty. His denunciation of the priestly and

10 *Mistra Jana Husi Sebrané Spisy* (Praha, no date), III, 17.

monastic loose living is far more frequent than that of lay morals.

During those early years of his career, before he became acquainted with the theological views of Wyclif, the avowed objective of Hus's preaching, as has been already mentioned, was the reformation of the notoriously and incredibly corrupt life of the majority of the clergy, and the restoration of true religious zeal among the laity. Hus never stressed doctrinal reconstruction for its own sake, but always in connection with some effort at moral reform or religious awakening. He was driven, in course of time, to adopt many important modifications of the current doctrinal views. But this he did always from motives of practical application, not because of any speculative concern. Even the earliest of his *Postils,* comprising sermons preached during the first years of his ministry (1401), contain vigorous denunciation of the scandalous living of unworthy clerics.[11] In his *Postil* of 1405, Hus manifests even greater reforming zeal. There is no explicit mention of Wyclif in this earliest preaching of Hus, although the latter's influence upon his thought is already discernible.[12]

With an increase of the Czech leaders' acquaintance with the theological thought of Wyclif, the influence of the English Reformer became quite marked. Some of the most important of the university professors became out and out Wyclifites. Other members of the reform party—as for instance Jakoubek of Stříbro—[13]remained more closely connected with the leaders of the native reform. Jakoubek, for instance, throughout his literary career, remained to a large degree dependent upon Matthew of Janov, whom he often quoted verbally and extensively. Thus, for example, in his sermon, *Accipiebant spiritum sanctum,* Jakoubek quoted Janov's *Regulae* so much that but little of it is of his own composition. The same is true of a sermon preached a year later (1410) at the University, in which he drew extensively upon the same source.[14] Similarly, the sermon *Ecce*

[11] J. Sedlák, *Studie a texty* (Olomouc, 1914-15), II, 394-399.
[12] *Ibid.*, 403.
[13] Known generally in non-Czech literature as Jacobellus of Mies.
[14] Sedlák, *Studie,* I, 374 and 376.

mulier is a compilation from Janov.[15] Jakoubek's tractate, *Libellus de Antichristo,* is almost altogether dependent upon Milíč and Janov. But despite this considerable dependence upon the older Czech Reformer, Jakoubek was likewise an enthusiastic disciple of Wyclif. In fact, he went far beyond Hus in his support of the doctrine of the English Reformer, nor was he as discriminating in regard to Wyclif's doctrinal views as Hus always was. Despite all this literal dependence upon other reformers, Jakoubek never mentioned Wyclif, Janov, or Milíč by name.[16]

Accordingly, with the increase of the theological influence of Wyclif, the contemporary native reform movement underwent a radical transformation. It seemed almost to have absorbed the Englishman's views, or at least these latter gave it a new orientation. Consequently, the movement assumed to a considerable degree the Wyclifite character, and a large number of its adherents now became convinced and thoroughgoing disciples of the English Reformer. This remarkable change reminds one of a similar transformation which the native Russian revolutionary movement, dating back to the first quarter of the nineteenth century, had undergone within less than a century. It was so thoroughly transformed by Marxism that during the Revolution of 1917 the native element all but disappeared, and the foreign Marxian influence became the dominant force of the movement. Nevertheless, it would be a misrepresentation of the true character of the Czech Reformation to portray it as having had its inception and its substance in Wyclifism. Moreover, Hus never accepted the teaching of Wyclif without scrupulous discrimination, and remained to the end among the moderate adherents of the English Reformer. Others of his party went far beyond him in their espousal of the radical doctrines of Wyclif.

II

If this interpretation were generally accepted, there would have been no occasion for the present study. But such has not

[15] *Ibid.,* II, 462-77.
[16] Šimek, *Výklad,* I, xiii.

always been the case. This view has been summarily rejected by some historians, whose writings have become widely influential. With the publication of Wyclif's writings, not only has the dependence of Hus upon Wyclif been realized more clearly, but in the first flush of discovery it has been often grossly exaggerated. Hus's eminence in the apostolic succession of the native reform movement has been denied, and his thought has been declared to be a mere echo of Wyclif's. The book which more than any other contributed to this revolutionary change was Johann Loserth's *Hus und Wiclif: zur Genesis der husitischen Lehre*,[17] published in 1884. It created a sensation, and has influenced subsequent writing in the field. In his zeal to honor the great English thinker whose works he was editing, Loserth denied Hus all originality and well-nigh all importance. He charged Hus with mechanical and slavish appropriation of his English master's ideas, and asserted in regard to the writings of Hus that, "some of them entirely and others for the greater part, form the exclusive property of Wiclif, and . . . there is no ground for speaking of a Hussite system of doctine."[18] Discussing Hus's *De ecclesia,* Loserth has summarily affirmed—although without much concern for historical accuracy or justice—that "it is taken word for word" from Wyclif's treatise of the same name.[19] Similarly he has asserted in regard to Hus's *De indulgenciis* that: "From the defining of the indulgences onwards, everything is the property of the latter."[20] Loserth's thesis has been accepted to greater or less degree, without much attempt at verification, by a considerable number of subsequent writers. Thus owing to the undiscriminating judgment of this over-enthusiastic admirer of Wyclif, who permitted his zeal to run away with his discretion, the thought and work of the Czech Reformer have been considerably undervalued.

Since biographical research has not produced any important

[17] Its English translation, *Wiclif and Hus,* was published in London, the same year. A second German edition was issued in Munich and Berlin, 1925.
[18] *Ibid.,* xxx
[19] Johannes Wyclif, *Tractatus de ecclesia* (London, 1886), xxvi.
[20] Loserth, *Wiclif,* 141.

contribution to our knowledge of the life of Hus,[21] modern study since Loserth's day has been focused upon the interpretation and evaluation of his teaching. Accordingly, the two principal aspects of modern investigation of the subject comprise the relation of Hus to his reformist predecessors and contemporaries, particularly to Wyclif, and the elucidation of the true character of his own doctrinal views. These two phases of the subject will serve as the foci of the present study.

[21] The most recent brief biography, summarizing the latest research, may be found in an article written by Kamil Krofta, in *Cambridge Medieval History* (New York, 1936), VIII. The most extensive treatment of the subject, comprising Hus's life and teaching is the Czech work by V. Novotný and V. Kybal, *M. Jan Hus, život a učení,* I[1-2], II[1-3] (Praha, 1919-1931). Indispensable source materials comprise: V. Flajšhans, ed., *Spisy M. Jana Husi,* 8 parts (Praha, 1903-1908), which contain his Latin works; K. J. Erben, ed., *Sebrané spisy české,* 3 vols. (Praha, 1865-1868); V. Novotný, ed. *Korespondence a dokumenty M. Jana Husi* (Praha, 1920); Jan Sedlák, *Studie a texty,* I-II (Olomouc, 1913-1915). Other valuable monographs: K. Krofta, *Listy z náboženských dějin českých* (Praha, 1936); O. Odložilík, *Wyclif and Bohemia* (Praha, 1937); O. Odložilík, *M. Štěpán z Kolína* (Praha, 1924); Jan Sedlák, *Mister Jan Hus* (Praha, 1915); F. M. Bartoš, *O Husa a o Husovi* (Praha, 1935); D. S. Schaff, *John Hus* (New York, 1915); D. S. Schaff, ed., *John Hus's De ecclesia* (New York, 1915); F. Lützow, *The Life and Times of Master John Hus* (London, 1909); E. J. Kitts, *Pope John the Twenty-Third and Master John Hus of Bohemia* (London, 1910); John T. McNeill, *Makers of Christianity,* (New York, 1935, II, ch. VI, pp. 166-174; R. R. Betts, "English and Czech Influences on the Husite Movement," in *Transactions of the Royal Historical Society,* xxxi (1939).

II
THE WYCLIFISM OF HUS
I

LOSERTH'S charges, echoed in the writings of others who followed him in his estimate of Hus, may be conveniently grouped under two general headings: in the first place, the charge of extensive literary plagiarism consisting of unacknowledged, word for word excerpts from the works of Wyclif; secondly, the denial of all originality of Hus's thought and the affirmation that his doctrinal views are essentially identical with those of Wyclif. In other words, he asserts that Hus's system of thought is a mere cock boat tugged behind in the backwash of a mighty galley—Wyclif.

In regard to the first charge, Loserth proceeds to prove his thesis by the laborious, quantitative, and seemingly fair and scholarly method of citing parallel passages from the writings of the two reformers. He builds up his argument with painstaking, pedantic punctilio. But as Chesterton would say, the learned author displays more than normal ingenuity in missing the point. Loserth's severe judgment of Hus rests frankly upon his application of the present-day literary standards to the age of scholasticism. For our age, it is doubtless a reprehensible practice to quote passages from another author's writings without giving him due credit. Hus is indeed guilty of such a practice, for as a matter of fact he seldom mentions Wyclif by name, although in the true scholastic fashion his writings otherwise fairly swarm with quotations from such acknowledged authorities as Augustine, John Chrysostom, Gregory the Great, Gratian, Bernard of Clairvaux, and Peter Lombard. But it must be remembered that quoting Wyclif by name was like waving a red rag before a bull: the study of Wyclif's theological works had been repeatedly forbidden, and it would have been plainly unwise to defy the authorities needlessly. Even so, Hus occasionally does cite the name of the English Reformer.

But the harsh verdict of Loserth loses much of its apparent justification when one remembers the literary standards of medieval scholastics. Even upon a superficial acquaintance with their productions it is clear that originality was by no means regarded generally as a virtue. It would be a mere commonplace to assert that many medieval theological writers were essentially compilers of currently acknowledged authorities, nor did they always take the trouble to indicate the sources from which they had culled their material.

Examples of such practices are not difficult to find. As for the very early writers, one may recall with profit the advice given by St. Augustine to preachers not gifted with unusual mental powers. He counselled them to memorize what had been written by their intellectual superiors and thus regale their audiences with good, if not original, sermons.[1] This advice did not fall upon deaf ears, even outside the circle of preachers. Isidore of Seville and the Venerable Bede are notorious for the copious use they made of previous writers. H. O. Taylor says of Isidore that he habitually compiled his writings from the works of earlier authors "whether he says so or not." "No need to say that it contains nothing that is Isidore's own."[2] It has been only recently realized, that is, with the discovery in 1921 of the Lübeck MS. of Gerard Groote's *The Following of Christ,* how much of this work had been incorporated by Thomas à Kempis into his *Imitatio Christi.* The reason why the saintly Thomas had been given credit for the whole work was that he had not acknowledged his extensive quotations. Surely he was not conscious of having committed an unethical act![3] Moreover, it is well known that Francis Bacon appropriated much from Montaigne without taking the trouble explicitly to mention it. And what could

[1] "On Christian Doctrine," in *The Nicene and Post-Nicene Fathers* (Buffalo, 1887), II, 596.
[2] H. O. Taylor, *The Mediaeval Mind* (New York, 1919), I, 105.
[3] Joseph Malaise, S. J., ed., *The Following of Christ* (New York, 1937), xx-xlv. The mystical writings of the "Friends of God" and "The Brethren of the Common Life" present a notoriously difficult case in the matter of detecting their real authorship. Such is the case of a contemporary of Hus, Rulman Merswin; cf. R. M. Jones, *The Flowering of Mysticism* (New York, 1939), 122 ff.

one say of William Shakespeare and Ben Jonson! After all, "Drink to me only with thine eyes" was originally written by Philostratus, and as for Jonson's *Discoveries,* "he left it for the critics of a later age to track every chapter to its lair."[4] Jakoubek's practice in this respect has been already mentioned. Even Hus's revered teacher, Stanislav of Znojmo, leaned heavily upon Wyclif in his eucharistic treatises written in defense of the doctrine of remanence. He often excerpted whole passages verbally from the works of Wyclif.[5] The celebrated Chancellor of the University of Paris, Jean Gerson, who served as one of Hus's judges at the Council of Constance, published a tract, *Declaratio compendiosa defectuum virorum ecclesiasticorum,* which, with the exception of one section, was taken by him word for word from chapters xvi-xx of Henry of Langenstein's *Consilium pacis de unione et reformatione ecclesiae.*[6] The same practice was indulged in by Cardinal Pierre d'Ailly who, in expounding certain doctrines, "had copied almost literally from Ockham's *Dialogus,* without even naming the source."[7] Wyclif himself, for that matter, followed this common practice and freely copied from his predecessors. Workman says of him: "That we discover the knowledge (displayed by Wyclif) to be largely copious extracts from medieval textbooks, Gratian's *Decretum* and the like, may lessen our estimate of Wyclif's scholarship but should not detract from our conception of his influence. To the medieval mind it was precisely in such knowledge of textbooks and in the ability to bring to bear their authority in debate that true wisdom consisted."[8] The same author has also freely conceded Wyclif's dependence upon Grosseteste[9] and William of Pérault, of whose *Summa virtutum ac vitiorum* he had "incorporated many sections."[10] Similarly, chapter xx of Wyclif's *De ecclesia* was largely copied from St. Augustine.[11]

4 Ward and Waller, eds., *The Cambridge History of English Literature* (New York, 1933), IV, 396, 28.
5 Sedlák, *Studie,* II, 372.
6 J. B. Schwab, *Johannes Gerson* (Würzburg, 1858), 121.
7 P. Tschackart, *Peter von Ailli* (Gotha, 1877), 43.
8 H. B. Workman, *John Wyclif* (Oxford, 1926), I, 102.
9 *Ibid.,* I, 115.
10 *Ibid.,* I, 342.
11 *Ibid.,* II, 6, footnote 3.

A similar conclusion regarding Wyclif's dependence upon William of Pérault and Bishop Grosseteste was reached by Loserth himself, who printed the sections borrowed from older writers in parallel columns.[12] Several other examples, illustrative of the borrowing habits of such illustrious schoolmen as Alexander of Hales and Thomas Aquinas are given in the work of Bartoš.[13]

As Hus had quoted other writers in accordance with the convenient custom of the time, so later writers quoted him without troubling themselves about the formality of acknowledging their source. There exist two expositions of the *Pater noster,* composed shortly after the time of Hus by some unknown authors, who made considerable use of the two works of Hus dealing with the same subject.[14] It is interesting to note that Hus in turn had borrowed some of his material from Wyclif. How amusing it would be to learn from whom Wyclif had copied in this particular instance, if such should be the case!

Loserth's cavalier treatment of Hus did not pass unchallenged and unscrutinized. A Catholic scholar, who cannot by any stretch of imagination be accused of any undue bias in Hus's favor, and who in fact may be said to be leaning in the opposite direction, has provided evidence disproving Loserth's overstatements. This is Jan Sedlák, who has subjected a considerable portion of the total writings of Hus to a searching scrutiny in respect of Hus's literary sources, comparing them particularly with the writings of Wyclif. Although, unfortunately, he did not apply his test to all the writings of Hus, yet his results are exceedingly illuminating and fairly representative.

The chief work of Hus subjected to an analysis by Loserth is *De ecclesia.* Sedlák drew his own conclusions regarding this work, after an independent and far more thoroughgoing examination and comparison with Wyclif's *De ecclesia* and *De potestate papae.* He found that "although Hus copied whole paragraphs from Wyclif, still the compilation is relatively independent, and that the idea upon which he based his teaching

[12] J. Loserth, *Johann Wiclif und Guilelmus Peraldus* (Vienna, 1916).
[13] F. M. Bartoš, *Husitství a cizina* (Praha, 1931), 22-23.
[14] Sedlák, *Studie,* II, 438-45.

regarding the function of the church is his own. The second, polemical section, although ideologically it is an echo of Wyclif, but rarely coincides verbally with the latter. Altogether it is possible to trace to Wyclif less than one-eighth of the treatise of Hus."[15]

In a later study, in which Sedlák has compared Hus's *De ecclesia* with the entire corpus of Wyclif's writings, he has summed up his judgment as follows:

> From this analysis it is evident that it is not possible to call the treatise of Hus, *De ecclesia*, plagiarism, although the work shows dependence upon Wyclif. Hus did not follow one or two treatises of Wyclif, (*De ecclesia*, and *De potestate papae*), but gathered from Wyclif's literary corpus everything which dealt with the subject, and arranged it in a relatively independent whole . . . It is true that throughout the work, both in the first, systematic part, and the second, polemical part he operates with Wyclif's concepts, which he copies in long excerpts from the latter's treatises. But he never follows any one of these exclusively, nor does he follow Wyclif's order of treatment. Accordingly, Hus's treatise *De ecclesia* is a fairly competent and independent compilation from the writings of one author, to be sure, and one whom Hus never names, but from works which in the published form amount to thirty-six volumes! That is certainly a piece of literary work which should not be underrated![16]

Sedlák's comparison of other works of Hus with those of Wyclif and of others confirms the evaluation arrived at on the basis of *De ecclesia*. Thus, for instance, when in partial fulfillment of the requirements for the bachelor of divinity degree Hus was obliged to deliver lectures on Lombard's *Sentences*, he had to follow, according to the requirement, some acknowledged master, for he was not allowed to expound his own views. Whom did he choose? In composing the third book, he followed for the most part Wyclif's *De benedicta incarnatione*.[17] In the second part of the work, he followed Wyclif's *Decalogus*, although he copied relatively little from it. But Hus showed himself exceedingly skillful in the use of excerpts, avoiding, as he did in all which he adopted from his English teacher, all passages which were theologically of dubious orthodoxy or altogether heterodox.[18] It is in such masterly skill in the use of just what

---

[15] *Ibid.*, I, 170-1.
[16] *Ibid.*, II, 526-7.
[17] *Ibid.*, I, 436.
[18] *Ibid.*, I, 448.

was acceptable that Hus's independence of judgment may best be seen. Even when he used a direct quotation, Hus was critical enough to change an offending word or phrase and thus to draw the teeth of an otherwise non-orthodox meaning of the sentence. In the fourth book of his lectures, Hus abandoned Wyclif's lead altogether and chose other guides. He based his exposition on certain popular theological compendia of the time—the work of an Augustinian, Thomas of Strasbourg, entitled *Scripta super IV libros Sententiarum*, later published in Strasbourg in 1490; and the work of a Dominican, Hugo of Strasbourg, *Compendium*, which was likewise a widely-known handbook.[19]

In writing his most polemical Czech work, *Concerning Simony*, Hus based it partly on Wyclif's treatise of the same title. Out of the one hundred and fifty-four pages of the latter, only about eighteen were incorporated by Hus in his work, i.e., a little more than one-ninth of the entire text.[20] Accordingly, the greater part of the work, some nine-tenths of it, represents original composition. Chapter seven was modelled upon Wyclif's *De officio pastoralis*, about one and a half pages of it having been incorporated in Hus's treatise.[21] According to his invariable rule, Hus exercised great care in choosing only such passages as would fit into the frame of his own thought, and in avoiding everything which would lead him beyond his own doctrinal position. It is this consistent moderation of theological formulation, one might almost say this liberal scholasticism of Hus, which distinguishes him from the radicalism of Wyclif.

In his Latin treatise, *Expositio decalogi*, Hus followed the work of an Augustinian monk, Henry of Freimar (1318-54), Professor at Erfurt, entitled *Praeceptorium seu de decem praeceptis*.[22] According to Sedlák, the short version of the *Exposition of the Faith* represents "an almost literal translation" of Wyclif's sermon, *Bene omnia fecit*."[23] But Novotný regards Sedlák's reasoning in this instance as unconvincing. According to the

[19] *Ibid.*, II, 125-31.
[20] *Ibid.*, I, 179.
[21] *Ibid.*, I, 305.
[22] *Ibid.*, I, 24.
[23] Wyclif, *Sermones*, I, 291-7.

former, the shorter version of the *Exposition of the Faith* is an abbreviation of the longer version which of course was composed prior to the shorter version. It would seem unreasonable to hold that Hus would have used a sermon of Wyclif in order to condense a longer work of his own. The longer version of the *Exposition of the Faith,* the *Decalogue,* and *the Lord's Prayer,* are among the most important of the Czech writings of Hus. In their composition, he availed himself of the writings of Hugo of Strasbourg to some extent, and of some works of Wyclif. Novotný estimates that the *Exposition* is about one-third, and the *Decalogue* about one-half, translations from other writers, mostly from Wyclif.[24]

The erratic and eccentric character of Loserth's arithmetic may be easily detected in his computation of Hus's dependence upon Wyclif in his *De indulgenciis.* He has ascribed almost the whole work to Wyclif.[25] But when he printed the two treatises side by side, on his own showing it appears that only nine half-page columns were copied from Wyclif, although the treatise of Hus comprises twenty full pages.[26] Moreover, Kybal does not allow even this much as demonstrably dependent upon Wyclif's text, and asserts that some of the material cited must be excluded.[27]

The collection of Hus's vernacular sermons, which goes under the name of the *Czech Postil,* is also indebted in some parts and to some degree to Wyclif, although many sermons of Hus are of original composition. The amount of text taken over, some almost verbally (i.e., in translation), constitutes about one-tenth of the whole work. However, the translation is never mechanical, but always adapted, modified.[28] But it must be remembered that since many manuscripts of Wyclif's works have been found in Prague or elsewhere in Bohemia, it is by no means certain whether some sermons of Hus have not been ascribed to Wyclif, and *vice versa.* As a matter of known fact, some works of other

[24] Novotný, *Jan Hus,* II, 195.
[25] Loserth, *Wiclif,* 141.
[26] *Ibid.,* 236-246.
[27] Vl. Kybal, *M. Jan Hus* (Praha, 1926, 3 vols.), II², 18, footnote 1.
[28] Sedlák, *Studie,* I, 282.

Czech Wyclifites have actually been included in Wyclif's published works as his own.[29] Nevertheless, in Sedlák's opinion, Wyclif's *Sermones* were drawn upon in the composition of some shorter treatises of Hus as well as of some sermons. He asserted that the fourth chapter of Hus's beautiful exhortation to a life of ascetic piety and virtue, entitled *The Daughter,* had been for the largest part literally translated from a sermon of Wyclif.[30] The remainder of the work he regarded as original. But Novotný disagreed with Sedlák's judgment in the matter, and has regarded the dependence of the fourth chapter of the treatise on Wyclif's sermon as very problematical and by no means proved. He has categorically rejected any idea of a literal translation, and has admitted only a possibility of a reminiscence of Wyclif's sermon on the part of Hus.[31] There are Latin sermons of Hus preached on various occasions after 1410 which were undoubtedly partly based on Wyclif. Thus the sermon *"Vos estis sal terrae"* was so largely reproduced from Wyclif that in Novotný's opinion Hus deliberately preached Wyclif's sermon, during the time when the struggle over Wyclif raged most fiercely, in order to show that some sermons of the latter were quite orthodox.[32] In another collection Hus actually presented a sermon of Bede, although he expressly and specifically stated so.[33]

This survey of the comparisons of the works of Hus with those of Wyclif, although incomplete, suffices to prove that Loserth has grossly exaggerated the verbal dependence of Hus upon the writings of the English Reformer. Bearing in mind the usual compilatory nature of scholastic compositions, Hus cannot be accused of "plagiarism" to a degree greater than that of other medieval writers. But to note what Hus transcribed from other writers, particularly from Wyclif, is of less importance than to observe what he left out. He invariably modified radical statements of Wyclif, so that even though the hands were Esau's,

[29] *Ibid.,* I, 171 and II, 200, footnote 2, asserts that the treatises included by M. H. Dziewicki in Wyclif's *Miscellanea philosophica,* II, 1-151 and 173-88, really belong to Stanislav of Znojmo and Stephen Páleč.
[30] Wyclif, *Sermones,* IV, 66-74; Sedlák, *Studie,* II, 359-66.
[31] Novotný, *Jan Hus,* I², 219, note 1.
[32] *Ibid.,* 490-491.
[33] *Sebrané spisy,* IV, 96-7.

the voice was Jacob's—even when the words were Wyclif's, the views were those of Hus.

II

Loserth's second charge is a concomitant of the first: that since the Czech Reformer had copied extensively and verbally from Wyclif's writings, his ideas were but a faint echo of those of his English master. To deal with anyone's "originality" is a notoriously difficult matter. Most of the concepts with which any thinker operates—as history of culture amply shows—have been appropriated from the cultural inheritance of humankind; his own contribution as a rule is relatively small. But there is something positively amusing in charging a medieval scholar with a lack of originality! Scholastics were scholastics just because to them originality was no such virtue as it is held to be by modern scholars. A faithful transmission of the knowledge of the past, at most a fresh commentary upon the ancient truth, came much closer to their notion of virtuous scholarly conduct! There are conspicuous exceptions to this statement, as everyone knows, but these do not invalidate the main thesis.

Wyclif was by no means as original as Loserth, by inference, would like to make him. To affirm that Wyclif's doctrinal system was—to use Loserth's language—"exclusively the property of Wyclif," is to undertake a great deal more than one can prove. For not even Loserth, in a self-contradictory fashion, denies that Wyclif derived many of his fundamental ideas from St. Augustine, Bishop Grosseteste, Archbishop Bradwardine, Archbishop Fitzralph, William of Pérault, Marsiglio of Padua, and William of Ockham.

Comparing Wyclif with the two last-named thinkers, who in their ecclesiology had put forth even a more radical program than Wyclif did, McGiffert sums up the relationship as follows:

Half a century later the Englishman John Wyclif followed Marsiglio and Ockham and even outdid them in attacking both the political and the spiritual supremacy of the pope. It is not necessary to reproduce his positions in detail. They were in the main identical with those of his predecessors.[34]

[34] A. C. McGiffert, *A History of Christian Thought* (New York, 1933), II, 350.

Wyclif, in fact, nowhere claims the originality which his enthusiastic admirers would thrust upon him.

The difficult task of evaluating the relative degree of dependence of Hus upon Wyclif may best be achieved by a study of the gradual influence of the English Reformer's theological views upon Hus, and the latter's reaction to them. In order to do this adequately, a brief résumé of the events which brought Hus to the leadership of the reform party, and thus in the eyes of its opponents made him responsible for the Wyclifite radical views held by some members of it, must be presented. Hus became acquainted with the philosophical writings of Wyclif in his undergraduate days, under the influence of his chief teacher, Stanislav of Znojmo. The latter was the acknowledged head of the philosophical school of realism at the University of Prague. This party comprised the majority of Czech masters, as against the nominalist German masters. Stanislav's views were so largely Wyclifite that his *De universalibus* deceived even the learned editor of Wyclif's works, who published it as Wyclif's own production.[35] Hus's acquaintance with the theological works of Wyclif came later. When the German masters of the University, on May 28, 1403, began their attack upon the theological teachings of the English realist, Wyclif, they presented to the University for condemnation the twenty-four articles which had already been rejected at the Blackfriars' Synod in London held in 1382. Besides, a Silesian master, John Hübner, augmented these by selecting twenty-one additional articles. This zealous savant, who at the time assumed the rôle of the chief antagonist of nascent Wyclifism in the University, had petitioned the chapter in Prague which was then administering the archiepiscopal office during a vacancy, for a judgment against the hated reform movement. The chapter requested the University for a preliminary advice in the matter. Since the German masters held the majority of votes, the meeting of the University resulted, as could be expected, in an indiscriminate condemnation of all the forty-five articles. It must be remembered that

[35] M. H. Dziewicki, *Miscellanea philosophica* (London, 1901-1903), II, 1-151, 173-188.

by a peculiar constitution of the University, that institution was composed of four "nations," the Bavarian, Silesian, Polish, and the Czech. Nevertheless, the Czechs had an undisputed numerical majority. But since each "nation" had a vote, the Czechs were certain to be defeated three to one on any issue on which the other three groups were fairly in agreement. Most of the Czech masters opposed this indiscriminate rejection of the theses *in toto,* not because they regarded them all as orthodox, but because they were not all heterodox, and because at least some of them had been given an incorrect meaning. Some masters held that the theses had been deliberately falsified by Hübner. The leaders of the Czech party, although inadequately acquainted with the doctrinal views of Wyclif—his theological works had just then gradually come to their notice—held that the forty-five theses did not correctly represent his teaching. It must be remembered that up to very recently only the philosophical writings of the English Reformer had been generally available. On this occasion, the chief rôle in the debate on the Czech side was played by Stanislav of Znojmo, with whom was associated a younger master, Stephen of Páleč. The latter was so confident of the impeccability of his beloved master in philosophy that he hotly challenged any and all in the gathering, holding up some work of Wyclif and crying: "Let anyone arise and attack even a single word of it, and I am willing to defend it!"[36] Stanislav also declared himself opposed to the branding of all the theses as "heretical, erroneous, and scandalous." In fact, in 1406, he went so far in his defense of Wyclif as to publish a treatise, *De corpore Christi,* in which he openly espoused the doctrine of the remanence of the material elements in the sacrament, on the ground that the church had not hitherto defined the doctrine dogmatically. In this assumption he was wrong, for remanence was presumably excluded by the Lateran canon on transubstantiation passed in 1215.

Hus, who was not among the leaders of the movement at the time, thereafter gave himself zealously to the study of the theo-

[36] Novotný, *Jan Hus,* I¹, 110.

logical works of Wyclif. In the end he gathered for his own private use probably most of Wyclif's writings. Considering the awe-inspiring extent of the works published by the Wyclif Society, this was no mean feat in itself! He had opposed the condemnation of the forty-five theses, along with the other Czech masters, not because he accepted them as representing his own convictions, but because he "feared to sin by condemning them as heretical, erroneous, or scandalous," as he expressed it later.[37] He became so proficient in the knowledge of Wyclif's views that he was probably chosen by the reform party to defend the English realist in the *quodlibet* held in January, 1404. But Hus made it plain that he opposed the wholesale condemnation of the forty-five theses only on the ground that they misrepresented Wyclif's true teaching.

Faithful to his reformist program, Hus, who in 1404 received the degree of *baccalarius cursor* after the usual five years of study, began his career by expounding Peter Lombard's *Sentences*. In these lectures are to be found the germs of his reformist emphases. They are cast in a form prescribed for such exercises —the scholastic hair-splitting, encumbered with endless distinctions and logical quibbles. Hus was not free to change this form, and this is probably the reason for the deadly monotony of the work. But occasionally he himself rebelled against some incredibly inane problem set for him in order to sharpen his acumen—such as whether angels are capable of paternity or maternity,[38] whether the heavens are in the form of a sphere or a barrel,[39] what would humankind be like if Adam had not sinned,[40] etc. Hus passed these by with a remark: "Let them sleep." The work as a whole gives one the impression that its author was scrupulously orthodox, accepting even in minute detail the current teachings of the church. Hus affirmed the Augustinian doctrine of original sin, but countered it by the equally

[37] V. Novotný, *M. Jana Husi korespondence a dokumenty* (Praha, 1920), No. 43, p. 124.
[38] *Sebrané spisy*, III, 195-96.
[39] *Ibid.*, 212.
[40] *Ibid.*, 233.

Augustinian teaching regarding baptismal regeneration.[41] He affirmed transubstantiation, and made no protest at this time against withholding the cup from the laity.[42] Intimations of the reformist program are clearly discernible in his assertion that although baptism and the sacrament of the altar may be validly administered by an unworthy priest, yet the latter sins grievously because he administers the sacraments unworthily; the layman who knowingly communes at the hands of a condemned heretic, schismatic, or fornicator, likewise commits sin.[43] The stand Hus took on the matter of excommunication he held to the end. He says: "It is impossible to excommunicate a man justly, unless he first and primarily excommunicates himself," i.e., by sinning mortally.[44] When an innocent man is excommunicated, he should suffer it humbly, and should rejoice that he has been deemed worthy to suffer for righteousness' sake. An ecclesiastical superior who sins may be reprimanded by his inferior, even a layman, although "with respect, in order that no prejudice arise as to his office."[45]

It is evident that Hus emphasised the moral character of the priestly office, rather than the sacerdotal. This betrays the native, rather than the Wyclifite, influence. As a corollary of this influence, he also felt that his preaching must not be arbitrarily interfered with, for it was a function commanded by God. No authority, if it be in conflict with God's commands, was to be obeyed.[46] These ideas were also held by Matthew of Janov. Since Wyclif's emphases corresponded so largely with those of the native movement, Hus was willing to accept the English Reformer as his master—but strictly with reservations.

Zbyněk Zajíc of Hasenburg, the Archbishop of Prague since 1402, despite his youth and inexperience, had enough insight into the sorry situation prevailing in the church and among the clergy to side at first with the reforming party. He even

[41] *Ibid.*, 264, 436.
[42] *Ibid.*, 452, 460–464.
[43] *Ibid.*, 440, 471.
[44] *Ibid.*, 490.
[45] *Ibid.*, 495.
[46] Novotný, *Jan Hus*, I¹, 133.

went so far as to appoint as the preacher at the clerical synod
of 1405 no less a person than the acknowledged head of that
party, Stanislav of Znojmo. In the autumn of the same year,
the preacher on a similar occasion was John Hus. This was
not an isolated instance, for Hus was to be the recipient of
similar honors on many subsequent occasions. This official favor
which the Archbishop bestowed upon the preacher of the Bethlehem Chapel protected the latter from the attacks of the enemies
of reform, who otherwise would certainly have found means of
silencing him. The good will of the royal court, particularly
of the Queen, Sophia, likewise shielded him from harm.

The synodical sermon of 1405 was an exceedingly severe
diatribe blazing with scathing denunciations of clerical abuses;
these included what the average anti-reformist priest undoubtedly regarded as mere pecadilloes. Hus particularly denounced
priests guilty of sexual irregularities, and demanded their un-
frocking and excommunication. He vehemently attacked the
current practices of "fleecing" the sheep by the shepherds from
the pope to the least altar-priest, and was particularly severe
on the monks for their money-grubbing. In his synodical sermon
of 1407 Hus repeated his attack upon the lax morals of the clergy,
and attacked the custom of demanding payments for sacraments.
It is not difficult to imagine the hot resentment against the radical
reformer on the part of the majority of the priesthood. Prophets
and reformers are a proverbially difficult lot to live with! What?
Shall the priesthood suffer such tongue-lashing in silence? Shall
it permit the zealot to cast the fees for the sacraments into their
teeth? Is is not written: thou shalt not muzzle a threshing ox?
A trifle inelegant, perhaps, to compare themselves with an ox,
but useful to muzzle with it that bellowing bull of Bashan! No
wonder that a few years later the clergy of Prague lodged a
complaint with the Archbishop in which some of the charges are
reminiscent, in a garbled form, of these synodical sermons.

The powerful anti-reformist party did not fail to try its
strength. Its first attempt was made in 1405 at the archiepiscopal court against Stanislav of Znojmo, who was charged with

heresy—the teaching of remanence. The Archbishop Zbyněk, who had been secretly denounced at Rome for tolerating heresy, had no other recourse but to appoint a committee to investigate the charge. Called before this body, Stanislav asserted that he did not hold remanence as an article of his personal faith, but had incorporated it in his treatise for the purpose of academic discussion. Moreover, he claimed that his work was in an unfinished state, and that it lacked the conclusion in which his own opinion regarding the doctrine would be properly set forth. The committee accepted the explanation as satisfactory, with the proviso that in the concluding part of his work he uniquivocally affirm his faith in transubstantiation. Accordingly, Stanislav was obliged to "complete" his treatise, that is, to deny remanence. Thereupon, the charge against him was dismissed.

Under these circumstances, the Archbishop now (June, 1406) felt impelled to prohibit publicly the defense of remanence in any form. But queerly enough, his formulation of the orthodox dogma was technically incorrect, for he insisted that after the consecration of the host, *nothing* but the body and blood of Christ remains. According to the official dogma, the accidents of the elements remain, although the substance is changed.

Jakoubek, Hus, and other members of the reform group were deeply disappointed with Stanislav's unheroic conduct, even though Hus did not share the latter's views. It was possibly the feeling that the reform party had lost face which actuated Hus to compose a treatise, *De corpore Christi*. In this small work, Hus does not explicitly name the Archbishop or refer to his proclamation. In the first part, which forms the bulk of the treatise, he discusses what the sacrament is not. He affirms, in the first place, that it is proper to speak of it as "bread," citing Christ's own words for the usage. However, it is not material, but transubstantiated, bread. Accordingly, it is not the physical body of Jesus Christ which is broken or eaten, or seen or touched, in the sacrament. The accidents of material bread remain unchanged, although its substance is changed. Accordingly, the unrepentant and unworthy who partake of it may partake only of the accidents—the material bread—without actually communing with Christ. Only those who are inwardly prepared by repentance and faith partake spiritually of Christ.[47] Thus just as Hus's teacher, Stephen of Kolín, had done three years earlier,[48] Hus refused to follow Wyclif on this dangerous ground, but also refused to accept Zbyněk's definition. His friend, Jakoubek, likewise published a treatise, *Confiteor antiquam fidem,* in which he frankly espoused the doctrine of remanence. This again proves Hus to have been a comparatively conservative member of the reform party, for others went far beyond him in their advocacy of Wyclifism. In this connection it is interesting to observe that in his *Exposition of the Revelation of St. John,* written during 1420-21, Jakoubek's remanentism is nowhere explicitly mentioned. In fact, in some references he could be understood as denying it. He stressed the importance of frequent communion—one of the chief emphases of Janov's reform program—and advocated admitting even infants to communion. Of course, by this time he strongly insisted on granting the cup to the laity. If one may be permitted to interpret the strange silence of Jakoubek regarding remanence as a change of mind on his part, then it would be clear that he followed Hus in this respect.[49]

Nevertheless, the Archbishop continued to show favor to the reformists, as is apparent from the appointment of adherents of this group to the influential post of the synodical preacher. Accordingly, the reformist sentiments, and even radical Wyclifite views, were freely disseminated under what appeared to be the Archbishop's own auspices and protection.

The equivocal stand of Stanislav had an adverse effect upon his leadership of the party. Although Stephen Páleč was still regarded as the more important and influential among the chief figures of the movement, Hus was slowly gaining in general regard and popularity. This was partly in consequence of the

---

[47] V. Flajšhans, ed., "De corpore Christi," in *Mag. Jo. Hus Opera omnia* (Prag, 1904), I, fasc. 2.
[48] O. Odložilík, *M. Štěpán z Kolína* (Praha, 1924), 20.
[49] F. Šimek, *Výklad,* I, lxxvi, lxxv.

death of a number of the older members of the group, such as Stephen of Kolín and Peter of Stoupno, who had died during 1406-7. By the latter year, Hus already was acknowledged as sharing the honors of leadership with Stanislav and Páleč. This was particularly true after one of the German masters of the University, Ludolf Meistermann, contrary to the generally observed custom of referring academic disputes to the University itself, sent an accusation of heresy against Stanislav and Páleč to the Roman curia. The accused men failed to secure a recall of the trial, and in the autumn of 1408 were compelled to risk the expensive and dangerous trip to Rome. Pope Alexander V freed the two Czech masters from the Bologna prison into which they had been thrown by Cardinal Balthassare Cossa. But as the price of freedom they had to recant Wyclif's teaching. Stanislav returned from Rome a changed man: from an advanced reformer he became a timorous conservative, and gradually both he and Páleč passed into the camp of the most vehement opponents of the reform movement. Merciful fate spared Stanislav from sharing with Páleč the despicable rôle of the most formidable enemy of Hus at the trial before the Council of Constance, for he had died prior to that event.

The next step in the development which in the end was to involve Hus in a conflict with the Archbishop and thus to deprive him of the latter's favor and to turn Zbyněk into a determined and unscrupulous enemy, was the charge of heresy levelled against a young master of arts, Matthew of Knín, a pupil of Stanislav and Hus. Having been imprisoned in the archiepiscopal court, he was placed on trial for holding the doctrine of remanence, and was frightened into recanting his view. Since he was a member of the University, the Czech masters shortly afterwards, on May 20, 1408, took action at the request of the Archbishop, once more agreeing that no one of their number might hold Wyclif's forty-five articles "in their heretical, erroneous, and scandalous" sense. Besides, only masters were allowed to read the *Trialogus, Dialogus,* and *De corpore Christi.*[50]

[50] Novotný, *Jan Hus,* I¹, 221.

Thereupon, in July the Archbishop renewed and expanded his prohibition of the teaching of remanence, and ordered that all masters, teachers, bachelors, and students who owned any of the works of Wyclif must present their copies "for correction" at the archiepiscopal court. King Václav, hitherto indifferent or passively favorable to the reform movement, was now beginning to feel incensed at the repeated occurrence of cases of heresy.

The order regarding the delivery of Wyclif's books was generally complied with. Hus delivered his copies to Zbyněk personally, with the request—which must have been made with the tongue in his cheek, since that prelate possessed no theological education—that the Archbishop mark the errors he should find! Since the reform party had complied with his two requests, the Archbishop had no reason to do otherwise than to make a public declaration, on July 16, 1408, that he had found no heresy in his archdiocese. He was actuated mainly by the King's insistence upon such a declaration for the sake of the reputation of the realm.

But this was a signal for the opponents of reform to redouble their efforts. In August, 1408, they lodged a formal charge against Hus in the archiepiscopal court. The accusing group consisted chiefly of some clergy of Prague who felt themselves aggrieved by, and consequently protested against, Hus's denunciation of the priestly custom of demanding a special payment, particularly from the poor, for confession, the administration of sacraments, funerals, and other clerical functions. Hus was said to have asserted that any priest who made such charges was a "heretic." If this charge was based on his synodical sermons of 1405 and 1407, then we know that it was incorrect, for Hus had called the practice "simony" and "heresy of simony," which it actually was. Among the three charges against Hus, no accusation of heresy was included—how eagerly would his opponents have made it if they could!—but at least they claimed that Hus had expressed his wish on one occasion that his soul might be where Wyclif's was. Nevertheless, the accusers, without naming anyone, vaguely charged that "remanence is still held by many in this parish." That is the worst they could bring against the Reformer![51]

Hus promptly returned a detailed reply to the accusation, from the tone of which one might suspect him of almost making fun of it![52] In the first place, he assured the Archbishop that "whatever the Lord Jesus Christ and his church catholic desire to be believed, that I firmly believe." Thereupon, he presented five rebuttals of the first charge of his accusers, branding it a lie for the greatest part, although upholding the thesis that it is improper to *demand* payment for sacraments. But no less a person than the illustrious Peter d'Ailly had likewise advocated the abolition of fees for sacraments. As for the specific whereabouts of Wyclif's soul, Hus explained—in a manner clearly implying the Augustinian dictum that no one can be certain of his particular predestination—that he hoped it were in eternal blessedness: for "he did not dare to condemn anyone who had not been condemned by the Scriptures or the church instructed by revelation." He contended that to adjudge a man worthy of hell without any positive knowledge on which to base the judgment were not proper for a good Christian. When delivering his lectures, *Super IV sententiarum,* Hus returned to this charge, and answered it more fully. He said:

> This I expounded for the sake of those who with precipitate judgment and with certainty assert and preach that Master John Wyclif is eternally damned in hell. But I, wishing to avoid such precipitate judgment, hope that he is of the number of those predestined to salvation. Accordingly, if he be in heaven, may the glorious Lord who placed him there be praised! But if he be in the purgatory, may the merciful Lord deliver him quickly! But if he be in hell, may he remain in the everlasting punishment in accordance with the righteous judgment of God.[53]

Although the charge had been adequately answered on this occasion, it nevertheless made its appearance, along with the rest of the accusations, at the trial before the Council of Constance, where it did its work of prejudicing the minds of the judges against Hus.

[51] F. Palacký, *Documenta Mag. Joannis Hus* (Prague, 1869), 153-55.
[52] Novotný, *Korespondence,* No. 12, p. 30-41.
[53] *Super IV. sententiarum,* IV, dist. XX, 3, in V. Flajšhans, *Mag. Jo. Hus Opera omnia* (Prague, n. d.), II, 621.

Returning now to Hus's reply to the charges of 1408, and referring to the sly remark about the many who still held the doctrine of remanence, he requested the Archbishop "that your paternal grace might take notice of it and order these adversaries to designate and point out those remanentists." Obviously, he had no fear of being implicated. He summed up his reply by branding the first charge as a lie; the second as an incorrect statement; while the third he denied outright.

It was not difficult to demonstrate the puerility of the charges of the priests on the occasion of their presentation in 1408. But the important point to note in summing them up is that the accusations against Hus were directed against his reform efforts, against his denunciation of clerical abuses, and not against any supposed heretical opinions of his. Novotný's remark that "it was not . . . Wyclif who caused the total estrangement between Hus and the Archbishop, but the great ecclesio-political question,"[54] the question of the termination of the Great Schism, is as pertinent as it is discerning.

Despite this setback, the ill success of the accusers did not discourage them. They now determined to trap Hus in some compromising statement, and for that purpose one of the priests, John Protiva, who in fact had been a predecessor of Hus in the Bethlehem Chapel, assumed the office of a spy. Hus knew of it, and on one occasion addressed him directly from the pulpit, bidding him to write down what was said and carry it to his fellows. In this way, in 1409, Hus was once more accused before the Archbishop, who in this instance turned the matter over to the inquisitor, Master Mařík Rvačka. The accusations purported to comprise statements of Hus ranging from 1399 to 1409.[55] This document was the first to include charges of heresy, such as Donatism and remanence. The former accusation asserted that as early as 1399 Hus had said in the home of the priest of the Church of St. Michael in the Old Town that "a priest in mortal sin cannot transubstantiate the sacrament of

[54] Novotný, *Jan Hus*, I[1], 269.
[55] Palacký, *Documenta*, 164-169.

the holy body of Christ, nor can he administer other church sacraments." The answers given by Hus to the inquisitor, which by the latter's command were restricted to a curt yes or no, are not extant. But five years later Hus wrote a more extended answer to these charges of 1409, and in that version his answer was a categorical denial of the accusation, and an affirmation of the orthodox view that the validity of the sacrament does not depend upon the character of the officiating priest.

The dangerous charge of remanence was formulated as follows:

> Furthermore, it is charged that after many disputes he said and was not ashamed to affirm: "Do you want to know what I assert? That if a priest celebrating the mass is in God's grace, he effects the consecration of the bread so that under the form of bread there is the body of Christ. But if he is without the grace of God, then he effects nothing, for there is neither the body of Christ nor the consecrated bread, but it remains bread as it was before, even after the pronouncement of the words."

This charge is a skillful blending of the Donatist dictum that the character of the officiating priest determines the validity of the sacrament, with the Wyclifite tenet of remanence. It must be remembered that it was actually held at the time by the Lombard Waldensians, whom Jakoubek later attacked because of it.[56] As such it was brought against Hus for the first time. To it he bluntly replied that Protiva had lied.

Besides, the accusations comprised various alleged pronouncements of Hus against ecclesiastical authorities, as well as those presented to the Archbishop during the previous year, including the one regarding the whereabouts of Wyclif's soul. Most of them figured regularly in the later charges against Hus, particularly those drawn up in Constance, despite the fact that the Prague inquisitor must have dismissed them as unfounded, since he had taken no further steps against Hus. In fact, he had given Hus an official statement attesting his orthodoxy.

The circumstances which led to an aggravation of the Great Schism and indirectly resulted in such dire consequences for Hus, are sufficiently well known not to require any detailed

[56] Šimek, *Výklad*, I, lxxxiv.

exposition. King Václav of Bohemia gave adherence and support to the program of the revolted cardinals of Gregory XII.
They undertook to call a council which should terminate the
schism. Václav's interest in the matter centered upon his re-
covery of the imperial title, of which he had been deprived in
1403. Pope Gregory had recognized as the rightful emperor
Václav's rival, Ruprecht. Accordingly, the Czech King expected as the price of his adherence to the program of the revolted cardinals his restoration to the imperial dignity. Such
was the political aspect of the royal policy regarding the Council
of Pisa.

The Czech masters, among whom Hus naturally occupied
a position of influence, sided with the King in the matter of the
proposed council. The Archbishop, however, remained loyal to
his oath of office and supported Pope Gregory. Thus Zbyněk
drifted into opposition not only to the King, but also to the
reform party. It was this unfortunate circumstance of ecclesiastical politics which caused a rift between Zbyněk and Hus. The
former now felt compelled to seek support of the anti-reformist
clergy for his anti-royal policy, and in return to accede to their
program for the destruction of the hated reform movement. The
method adopted for that purpose was the only weapon which
could not fail to crush the reformers—an accusation of heresy,
a charge of Wyclifism. Zbyněk now lost no time: having decided upon the course, he immediately sent a request to Pope
Gregory for an approval of his steps against the Wyclifites,
particularly the burning of the books of Wyclif delivered by
their owners to the archiepiscopal court.

When the question of the refusal of obedience to Gregory
came before the University, the Czech masters supported the
measure, but the German masters disapproved it. When the
King, to his great chagrin and wrath, learned of the intransi-
gence of the Germans, he was so incensed that he was led to
issue the famous edict of Kutná Hora (better known as Kutten-
berg, the city where he was staying at the time), radically sub-
verting the constitution of the University by ruling that the

Czech nation, comprising the numerical majority, henceforth should possess three votes, while all the rest of the nations should have in common only one. This caused a veritable fury among the German masters who, after an attempted resistance to the royal mandates, finally left the country *en masse*. Their emigration resulted in the founding of the University of Leipzig. Although this Czech "victory" cannot be credited to Hus, the German hatred was focused upon the "heretical" Czech Reformer and contributed not a little to the prejudice and slander with which he was later treated at Constance.

Let us return to the subject of the Wyclifite books: Zbyněk decided to make use of this episode to inflict chastisement upon the reformers. He repeated his order that all the works of Wyclif be surrendered to him. When the term set for their delivery had expired, he issued a ban against all who still retained copies of the works of the English Reformer.

But Zbyněk soon realized that ultimately he could not withstand the King, if he would stubbornly continue to adhere to a policy so diametrically opposed to the latter's. King Václav could not permit the Archbishop to thwart his will. Moreover, Zbyněk had been in the meantime cited to Rome by the Pisan Pope, Alexander V. Seeing inevitable defeat staring him in the face, since the King had actually confiscated the archiepiscopal estates, Zbyněk capitulated, and on September 2, 1409, acknowledged the jurisdiction of Pope Alexander V. Thereupon, he was reinstated in his office and possessions.

By this act of submission the situation was radically changed: to secure the good will of Archbishop Zbyněk, whose pride had been not a little hurt by the forcible means of conversion to the royal policy, the Pope was now willing to accede to the Archbishop's requests, and to approve the latter's antireformist policy. Accordingly, Alexander ordered that all who had failed to surrender the works of Wyclif be subjected to the strictest punishment, and that preaching be restricted to the cathedral, monastic, and parochial churches, since it was by means of preaching that the Wyclifite doctrines were commonly spread. In fact, the latter prohibition was secured by the zeal of Zbyněk's delegates to the papal curia. They, as members of the anti-reformist party, were particularly anxious to silence effectively the bitter denunciation of their own misdeeds on the part of Hus and other reformers, and also wished to render any possible reconciliation between Zbyněk and Hus out of the question.

Fortified with the papal decree, the Archbishop ordered, on June 16, 1410, the burning of Wyclif's works surrendered to him by their owners—amounting to some two hundred manuscripts—and among them treatises of purely philosophical or pedagogic character. He also forbade the preaching of the erroneous articles, as well as all preaching whatsoever in "private" churches, including, of course, the Bethlehem Chapel. No wonder that the streets resounded with the taunting skit:

> *Bishop Zbyněk, A.B.C.,*
> *Burned books, though ne'er knew he,*
> *What was in them written . . .*

Thereupon, a storm of protests broke out. The University promptly and openly condemned the Archbishop's hasty act. That all the surrendered works of Wyclif—philosophical as well as theological and miscellaneous—should be condemned as heretical (the papal condemnation and burning of Wyclif's writings at Rome took place much later, on February 10, 1413) was clearly irregular. For after all, the philosophical writings were freely used at many universities as textbooks. The opposition to the burning of the books was based on the lack of discrimination as to the character of the various books condemned to the pyre. Some were purely philosophical and contained no dogmatic error. Zbyněk had full authority to forbid the errors contained in Wyclif's books, but not to prohibit the teaching of what was sound. Why not likewise burn Aristotle, who said that God did not create the heavens and the earth? Why not burn Lombard's *Sentences,* "which contain many errors?"[57]

[57] *Historia et monumenta,* I, 107.

Hus was now driven into an overt act of revolt: he defied the authority of the Archbishop regarding the prohibition of preaching in "private" chapels, and boldly continued to occupy the pulpit of the Bethlehem Chapel. He did so after appealing, along with his friends, from the decision of the Archbishop to Pope John XXIII, who had in the meantime succeeded Alexander V.[58] He explained this act of disobedience in his *Exposition of the Decalogue* as follows:

> Having placed these saints and Christ the God before my eyes, I did not consent to obey Pope Alexander and priest Zbyněk, the Archbishop, that I should not preach the Word of God. . . . The Word of God says: 'Preach the word to all the world.' But their commands are to the contrary: Do not preach the word to all the world . . . Know accordingly that you are not bound (to obey) except in such matters in which you are bound by obedience to God, for in such matters you should obey both evil and good lord or elder. Not as if you obeyed him (the lord), but as obeying God, whom all creatures obey. . . . Thus we should obey evil prelates or rulers in all matters and burdens which are not sinful. Such are all burdens which the faithful bear for Christ's sake. But we must not obey wrong commands which are against the commandment and counsel of Jesus Christ.[59]

Hus concluded that in this particular case the words of the apostles applied: "We ought to obey God rather than men." Accordingly, he resolutely went on preaching.

When Hus publicly read from the pulpit of the Bethlehem Chapel his appeal to the Pope, despite Zbyněk's ban on all who had previously appealed from his decision to the papal curia, the audience broke out into a loud approval, particularly when

---

[58] Novotný, *Korespondence*, 56-69. Dated June 25, 1410. In the *Postil* of 1413, in a sermon on the prohibition of plucking the tares, Hus refers to these events of three years before as follows: "and they (the prelates) openly confirmed it when they secured from Pope John XXIII a bull in which he openly commanded them to burn both the good and the bad books of John Wyclif. They (the books) irked them greatly, for they dealt with their simony, pride, fornication, and avarice. They are most incested because he (Wyclif) calls them almoners, and that they should not rule like secular lords. Also, because he writes that when priests live evilly and refuse to abandon the evil, seculars may take their property away for the purpose of depriving them of the means to sin, and that they should not give them tithes. These sayings were denounced by some doctors, canons, priests, and monks in the Prague City Hall. . . . But many masters stood up in the public hall of the college and proved from the Scriptures that the doctors with their cohorts cavilled at truth, and called upon those doctors to come to the school and prove (their contention) from the Scriptures. But they refused, for they dared not, having no scriptural basis for proving their derogation." *Sebrané spisy*, VI, 59.
[59] K. J. Erben, ed., *M. Jana Husi Sebrané Spisy České* (Praha, 1865), I, 91.

the heroic preacher declared his decision to defy the Archbishop by continuing to preach.

Zbyněk promptly excommunicated Hus for disobedience. This was another unjustified and flagrantly irregular action on his part, for Hus had not rejected the Archbishop's ecclesiastical jurisdiction, but merely had appealed from it to the curia whose final verdict he was ready to accept. To do so was his undoubted right.

Moreover, during the disputation held at the University on July 28, 1410, for the purpose of demonstrating disapproval of the Archbishop's indiscriminate condemnation of Wyclif, Hus himself defended Wyclif's treatise, *De Trinitate,* affirming that it contained no patent heresy or dogmatic error.[60] Jakoubek defended Wyclif's *Decalogus,* and again showed himself the most radical of the Czech Wyclifites, although at the same time a loyal adherent of the native reform movement. The defense of the elementary treatise on logic, *De probationibus propositionum,* which had likewise been burned, offered a splendid occasion for caustic wit of the disputants at the expense of the Archbishop. A little later Hus preached a sermon, *"Vos estis sal terrae,"* which consisted largely of direct citations from Wyclif's sermon on the same text, for the purpose of showing that the much-maligned Wyclif could preach a sermon not only dogmatically correct, but also effective and soul-stirring.[61]

It was at this time that Hus became the acknowledged leader of the reform party. Nevertheless, theologically he remained a moderate Wyclifite. He defended only Wyclif's reforms, not what passed in the eyes of orthodox churchmen for dogmatic errors. The Archbishop's reply to Hus's defiance was another accusation sent to the papal curia in which Hus was named as the leader of Wyclifism in Bohemia, although he was charged with no specific Wyclifite errors. The appeal which had been sent by Hus and some of his friends to the papal court was referred to a cardinal who requested the University of Bologna

[60] *Historia et monumenta,* I, 105 ff.
[61] Novotný, *Jan Hus,* I, 431; II, 490-91.

to express its opinion about it. The latter, of course, could not approve Zbyněk's hasty act of burning Wyclif's books indiscriminately, and censured the condemnation of the books on logic, philosophy, and morals. As for the theological books, it singled out a number of articles as not suitable for preaching or teaching. Thus in reality the contention of Hus was upheld and supported by this pronouncement.

The case of Hus at the curia took an unfavorable turn when King Václav's emissary, Dr. Jerome of Seydenberg, secretly went over to the side of the Archbishop and worked against the instructions he had received from the King. As a result, the Pope now referred the case to Cardinal Odo de Colonna, who rendered a decision in favor of Zbyněk (August 25, 1410). The Cardinal summoned Hus to answer the charges before him personally. It soon became known that the Archbishop presented the Pope and the investigating cardinals with horses and jewelry; the decision, therefore, need not cause any surprise.

Zbyněk now for the first time brought specific charges of heresy against Hus. He gathered testimonies of some clergy who affirmed that they had heard Hus defend heretical articles of Wyclif, particularly the doctrine of remanence, and the Donatist thesis that a priest in mortal sin does not consecrate validly. The Archbishop sent to the curia a man of notoriously dubious character, Michael de Causis, who was willing to use all the known legal tricks and dodges, fair or foul, to secure Hus's conviction.

, In the meantime, Cardinal Colonna, ignoring the appeal of Hus's legal representatives, pronounced the sentence of excommunication against Hus not on the ground of heresy, but of contumacy—non-appearance at the trial—(February, 1411).[62] The Archbishop then placed Prague under an interdict, extend-

---

[62] During the year 1413 Hus alluded to these events several times and gave his reasons for non-appearance. The most extensive of these is to be found in his *Postil of 1413*, where in preaching upon the text dealing with Jesus non-attendance of the feast at Jerusalem, he said:

"In the same way, I hope to God that I am excused for not presenting myself in Rome when I was cited before the pope. In the first place, I sent my representatives who for three years had been refused hearing: they were seized and imprisoned because they demanded justice. In the second

ing over the environs for two miles around. But even his own partisans did not always observe it. King Václav ordered that the interdict be altogether ignored.

It was in this way that the Archbishop turned from a defender and protector of Hus into his enemy. But Hus still enjoyed the King's favor, and in his turn he upheld the position of the King against the Archbishop. He cited Wyclif by name in connection with the latter's *De officio regis,* which affirmed the king's duty to protect the free preaching of the Word of God.

Pope John XXIII was not satisfied with Colonna's action and took the case out of his hands. Early in 1412 it was referred to Cardinal Zabarella, who under John's pressure—for at the moment the latter needed Václav's support—adopted a policy which boded ill for the Archbishop. Moreover, since the latter did not recompense the owners of Wyclif's works for their

place, the distance from Prague to Rome is greater than from the Lake of Tiberias to Jerusalem . . . In the third place, there is no command in the law of God (justifying) them to compel me to go to Rome in vain. In the fourth place, there is but little of God's truth at the papal court which they would administer according to God's law. In the fifth place, I would thus deprive the people of the (preaching of the) Word of God, . . . In the sixth place, I should spend a great amount of the alms given me by the people. In the seventh place, my contention is against papal customs and power, not that delegated by God, but invented by the devil. For Pope Alexander V for payment issued a bull in which he forbade the preaching of the Word of God to people in chapels, although these latter had been established and approved by popes for the purpose. It was also written in the bull that there should be no preaching anywhere except in parish (churches) and monasteries. This bull was secured by the Archbishop of Prague, the priest Zbyněk of good memory, along with other prelates. And the monk Jaroslav, a titular bishop, was a member of the delegation which went for the bull. It was also written in it that many hearts in the Kingdom of Bohemia and the Margravate of Moravia are infected by heresy, and that there is need of supervision and correction. Accordingly, that bull proves that both the Pope and the priest Zbyněk went contrary to the law: the Pope in granting, Zbyněk in securing, that the Word of God be not freely preached, which is contrary to the gospel and to the acts of our Savior, Jesus Christ, who had commanded the disciples to go into all the world, preaching the gospel to every creature. . . . Does then the bull conform to the Scriptures and the acts of Christ? Certainly not! Accordingly, I appealed to the Pope, but because the matter concerned even the present Pope, the truth was not granted hearing . . .

What good have they sought in forbidding the Word of God to be preached in chapels, or nowhere else except in parish (churches) and monasteries? There was jealousy, avarice, . . . and intention to deprive the Bethlehem Chapel of the Word of God. Other archbishops built chapels in order that preaching may be held in them: the Archbishop of Prague, the priest John, with his own hand, founded and approved the Bethlehem Chapel. Thus the late Zbyněk, having been instigated to it by the canons and the parish priests of Prague, as well as the monks who were of one mind with the priests regarding the Bethlehem (Chapel), desired to ruin the Chapel by depriving it of (the preaching of) the Word of God and thus to stop my

loss, as he had promised the King to do, Václav ordered the
sequestration of the incomes of the canons as well as of Prague
priests. In consequence, Zbyněk felt that luck had turned
against him. He was now willing to seek peace. His and
Václav's agents met, and Zbyněk professed himself ready to
submit to the King in return for the restoration of the temporalities. He professed willingness to write to the Pope and
to affirm positively that he knew of no heresy in his archdiocese;
he likewise promised to drop all lawsuits against Hus at the
curia, as well as to terminate the interdict. Thus the King secured a complete victory.

But Zbyněk's discomfiture proved too great to bear with
equanimity. Ignoring his promise, he did not annul the interdict,
nor did he write to the Pope in behalf of Hus, despite the fact
that the latter had presented Zbyněk with his *confessio fidei,*
fully orthodox in sentiment, in which he repudiated the charge
of remanence and every other heresy ascribed to him. Zbyněk
now fled from Prague, hoping to find refuge at the court of the

preaching altogether! For they agreed that if I desisted from preaching
in the Chapel in accordance with the Pope's command, the priests and
monks would not admit me to preach in any other place, for the papal
order left open only the parish (churches) and the monasteries. Having
perceived this, I stood up—with the aid of my merciful Savior—against
their unrighteous command and their clever wiles.

And finally, I did not go to the papal curia in order not to lose my life in
vain. For enemies abound everywhere, both Czech and German, seeking
my life: the Pope, my judge, is an enemy, the cardinals are enemies, as
is witnessed by their letters in which they called me a heretic, although
they have never heard nor seen me. For the Pope and the cardinals are
affected by the preaching against pride, avarice, and especially against
simony. . . . Moreover, false witnesses and their depositions made against
me in Prague were sent to Rome. One of these witnesses affirmed that
I preach that when a priest celebrates the mass, the body of God is not
present. Another bore witness that when a priest is in mortal sin while
celebrating the mass, he blesses the bread but there is no body of God.
Another bore witness that I preached that an old woman is worthier in all
respects than the Pope: and many other articles they falsely ascribed to me.
In the letter issued against me by the cardinal who was my first judge, I
was regarded as a false guide of the people and an originator of errors.
In the accusation of the priest Zbyněk, it was asserted by Michael, the priest
of the Church of St. Adalbert in New Town that all faithful Christians in
the Kingdom of Bohemia regard me as a heretic, and that I preach errors
and heresies every day in the Bethlehem Chapel, and that I am the prince
and the head of heretics. But not even that, I trust to God, will harm me,
nor do I feel resentful: for I know that priests did likewise to His holy
grace (Jesus), and that finally they tortured Him in an ignoble and cruel
death. To His holy grace I commit my contention that he might conclude
it as it pleases Him, even though it involve my rejection by men and death,
so long as He does not permit me to fall away from His truth." *Sebrané
spisy,* I, 103-105.

Emperor Sigismund. But death overtook him at Bratislava
(September 28, 1411). Thus the contest of Hus with the Archbishop, owing to the royal support, ended seemingly with the
victory of the reform party.

This success of the King's policy would have been more assured had it not been for the fact that Hus's case at the papal
curia was still unsettled, owing to Zbyněk's non-fulfillment of
his promise. King Václav was still personally favorably in-
clined toward Hus and the whole reform party among the Czech
clergy. For the time being, even the eventual condemnation of
Hus at the papal court need not be feared, for the royal support
was sufficient to protect Hus against the imposition of any serious
penalties. For despite the fact that the ban issued by Cardinal
Colonna had not been removed, nobody paid the slightest at-
tention to it. Moreover, Cardinal Zabarella had completely
reversed Colonna's judgment. Setting a new date for the trial,
he admitted the legal representatives of Hus to act in his behalf.
But this favorable turn of affairs was of short duration. Hus's
enemies secured the appointment of another judge, Cardinal
de Brancaiis; the representatives of Hus were then obliged to
leave the field to their opponents.

The King, of course, afforded the Czech reform party, of
which Hus was now the acknowledged leader, his protection
only so far as that party did not advocate any overt heresy.
For Václav was exceedingly jealous of the good name of his
realm. The constantly recurring charges of heresy hurled
against the reformers by their opponents were for the time being
recognized by the King as on the whole unfounded, as mere
calumnies resorted to in an effort to discredit inconvenient critics
of clerical abuses. Had Hus been more politic and worldly-
wise, he would have avoided at all costs any occasion which
might alienate the King's good will. But Hus regarded it as
his first duty to defend the truth as he saw it, irrespective of
consequences. This integrity of character, or lack of diplomatic
adroitness—if one wishes to look at it in that light—ultimately
alienated even the King's support. As with the aid of the court

4

of Frederick the Wise Luther defied the papacy, so could Hus likewise have ignored the ecclesiastical fulminations; but the loss of the support of the King was responsible for the defeat of the cause for which Hus and his party stood. That is the essential difference in the external circumstances which affected the course of the Czech and the German Reformations.

A series of incidents brought about the alienation of the King. In the first place, the charge of heresy was once more levelled against the Czech reform party, this time by an English scholar, a certain Dr. John Stokes of the University of Cambridge, who had come to Prague in September, 1411, as a member of a diplomatic mission. Some Czech university masters, naively assuming that the English scholar must be an admirer of Wyclif as they were, invited him to deliver a public discourse. But they mistook their man. Stokes not only refused the invitation to speak at the University, but expressed himself to the effect that anyone who had read Wyclif's books must in time necessarily became a heretic.

This was an insult, and as such was challenged by the reform party, Hus coming forth as its spokesman. He challenged Stokes to a public disputation at the University. But the Englishman again refused. Nevertheless, Hus delivered his address, *"Replica Magistri Ioannis Hus contra Anglicum Ioannem Stokes Vuicleffi calumniatorem,"* in which he defended Wyclif from the aspersion of heresy, although in that curious non-conclusive manner so characteristic of academic disputes: "I do not believe nor concede that Master John Wyclif is a heretic, although I do not deny it, either; but I hope that he is not a heretic, because in obscure matters it is proper to judge a man by assuming the better alternative. Therefore, I hope that Master John Wyclif is among the saved."[63]

This somewhat Quixotic defense of Wyclif was later utilized against Hus. At the Council of Constance, Stokes, who was present, not only charged Hus with being a thoroughgoing Wyclifite, but even testified that he had seen in Prague a treatise

[63] *Historia et monumenta,* I, 108.

ascribed to Hus which defended the doctrine of remanence. Despite Hus's denial, the testimony had a telling effect upon his judges, and proved in the end to add a fagot to Hus's pyre.

But the most important single incident, which had more decisive influence upon the King, and consequently upon the fate of Hus, than any other single event, was the Czech Reformer's determined and outspoken denunciation of the bull of indulgences. This was granted by Pope John XXIII in order to secure resources for the prosecution of his war with King Ladislaus of Naples. The bull was issued on September 9, 1411, but the plenipotentiaries for Bohemia were not named until in December. One of the two papal sellers of indulgences was the notorious Wenceslas Tiem, then Dean of Passau, whom Hus was to meet later among his most virulent accusers at Constance. Tiem farmed out whole archdiaconates, diaconates, and parishes for stated sums of money, and the unscrupulous renters were then left free to squeeze out of the people as much as they could. The open trading in forgiveness of sins carried on under Tiem's auspices was considered by the reform party and their adherents among the people as nothing less than sacrilegious. Similar nefarious practices connected with the conduct of the sales in 1393 had aroused Hus's teacher, Stephen of Kolín, to a vigorous protest and denunciation,[64] as a century later they were to arouse young Luther to the protest which marks the beginning of a new era in the history of western Christendom. On the occasion under consideration, they had a similar effect upon Hus. Even the timorous, and by this time quite conservative, theological faculty of the University could not approve the methods of Tiem. Hus later charged that "our doctors refused to answer the bachelors and students and to inform them when they had inquired in God's name whether they were in duty bound to obey the papal bull and to contribute to him (the Pope) out of the possession which God had granted them."[65] The Dean of the Faculty of Arts altogether refused to announce the sale.

---

[64] Odložilík, Štěpán, 37.
[65] Sebrané spisy, VI, 34-35.

Hus stated later than Stephen Páleč himself expressed the opinion that Tiem's indulgence proclamation contained "palpable errors."[66] No wonder that Hus, the acknowledged leader of the reform movement, could not keep silent. He poured out his indignation against the methods of the indulgence sellers in his sermons. He also published his reasons for the rejection of the methods used—although not of the doctrine of indulgence—in a special treatise.[67]

It was the King's attitude in the matter which led to tragic consequences for Hus. For reasons which are not fully clear, the King permitted the sale of indulgences in his domains, and thereafter any opposition to the sale was regarded by him as disobedience to his will. It was in this crisis that Hus's heroic faithfulness to truth dictated to him a course of action from which such men as Stanislav of Znojmo and Stephen Páleč shrank in fear. Hus knew that his defiance of papal authority, coupled with an opposition to the royal policy, spelled inevitable doom. But prudential considerations did not prevail with him. He "turned his face toward Jerusalem," or rather toward the pyre in Constance. He felt the deepest sorrow over the desertion of his former friends, who now turned into his bitterest enemies. But with his manly saying: "Páleč is a friend, truth is a friend: if both are friends, it is holy to give preference to truth,"[68] he unflinchingly went on his way.

But the protest of the theological faculty, of which Páleč was now dean, prevented any action on the part of the University authorities. Accordingly, Hus alone challenged all comers to a public disputation upon the theme of the bull of indulgences. Páleč made an effort to prevent the disputation by forbidding all bachelors of divinity—including Hus—to take part in it. Nevertheless, Hus proceeded to hold it before a large audience. He declared publicly that the faithful are not obligated to obey

[66] Palacký, *Documenta*, 223.
[67] "Quaestio Magistri Ioannis Hus, disputata ab eo . . . de indulgentiis siue de Cruciata Papae Ioannis 23, fulminata contra Ladislaum Apuliae regem," in *Historia et monumenta*, I, 174 ff.
[68] "Responsio Magistri Ioannis Hus, ad scripta M. Stephani Paletz theologiae doctoris," in *Historia et monumenta*, I, 264.

papal commands in case they contradict the law of Christ. Later, he addressed the clergy in a treatise[69] wherein he enumerated twelve reasons why the papal bull should be condemned: he particularly protested against the Pope's waging a war against Christians, and against the irregular and inadmissible abuse of the system of indulgences, the levying of a tax for the forgiveness of sins, and the total omission of all necessary spiritual presuppositions.

The theological faculty now took the field against Hus. They not only accused him before the King, but also published a declaration justifying and defending the papal indulgences. The situation was greatly aggravated when the opposition to the bull reached the stage of popular demonstrations, during which the Pope and his indulgence sellers were openly ridiculed. On one such occasion a copy of the indulgence bull was publicly burned on the square of the New Town. This in turn called forth a peremptory order of the King forbidding all opposition to the sale of indulgences. Wishing to put a stop to the ever-recurring heresy hunting, the King now ordered the theological faculty to prepare a dissertation which should disprove Hus's reasons against the sale of indulgences. This led to the publication of the pompous and bombastic *Tractatus gloriosus,* in which Hus's former friends and fellow-reformers went so far as to endeavor to cast the aspersion of heresy upon him. King Václav then called the two opposing parties to his castle of Žebrák. The conference yielded no positive results. The King thereupon insisted even more strenuously that the theological faculty refute the arguments of Hus. This drove Hus's former friends definitely into dogged defense of the papal system as it then existed, and thus utterly alienated them from the reform party.

In the meantime, a tragic occurrence brought about a crisis in the proceedings. Many openly protested in churches against the sale of indulgences, and this led to riots. Hus says that "when faithful Christians with good intentions warned priests

---

[69] "Contra bullam papae Ioan. XXIII," in *Historia et monumenta,* I, 189 ff.; also in V. Flajšhans, *Obrany v Praze* (Praha, 1916), I, 60-69.

against lying in their preaching, they were seized, beaten by the priests in the church, torn and buffeted, and then dragged into student hostels where they were whipped. The monks of the (monastery of the) Mother of God of the Snow in the New Town, and of other monasteries, conducted themselves similarly."[70] The crisis was reached when three young men, who had openly protested against the selling of indulgences carried on in a particularly revolting manner, in accordance with the recent royal command were seized and arrested. Hus and some masters protested against the arrest. Hus offered himself, as the real offender, to take the place of the three youths. But the aldermen pacified the deputation by assuring it that no serious punishment should be inflicted upon the three young men. Nevertheless, soon after Hus had left the officials, they ordered the three youths to be beheaded. The verdict was immediately carried out. An immense crowd gathered at the place of execution, and reverently carried the bodies of the dead to the Bethlehem Chapel. Now the reform movement had its "martyrs"! Henceforth, it ceased to be a predominantly academic affair, and became a popular movement. Hus had not taken part directly in the solemn services of burial, but soon afterwards preached a sermon in which he called upon all his hearers to permit no tortures to turn them from the truth.[71]

The people now, instead of being intimidated by the execution, were emboldened to protest against the sacrilegious trading

---

[70] *Sebrané spisy*, I, 112.
[71] In describing these stirring events in a sermon published in the *Postil* of 1413, Hus sums them up as follows: "And the originator of it all was Stephen Páleč, that doctor who at the time when he had loved truth had been my faithful and dear friend; and the second was Stanislav. They rose against us because we would not approve the papal bull in which the crusade was proclaimed—that is that whoever wishes, whether priests, nuns, and monks, may prepare themselves to exterminate King Ladislaus of Naples and all those who are subject to his power and who support him. In that bull he (the Pope) condemned him (King Ladislaus) to the fourth generation . . . and granted forgiveness of sins and of torments to all who should obey him or who should contribute money. Some risked their lives in the matter, as those who withstood the preachers who asserted that the pope is our earthly god and can grant forgiveness of sins and of torments to whomsoever he pleases, and that he should yield an iron sword like any secular prince. Of these (who withstood the preachers), Martin, John, and Stašek were beheaded, and were interred in the Bethlehem (chapel) in God's name. Others were seized, tortured, and imprisoned." *Sebrané spisy*, VI, 60.

in holy things. Arrests and whippings proved powerless to stop them. King Václav was so enraged with what he regarded as a rebellious disobedience of his orders that he was more and more confirmed in his growing aversion from the reform party. He ordered the University to gather at the Old Town Hall, where the theological faculty presented to the rest of the University its proposals which had been already approved by the King at the meeting at Žebrák. They comprised the prohibition, under pain of exile, of preaching of heresies, of opposition to the papal bull, of defending the forty-five theses of Wyclif, and of seven others formulated by the theological faculty. The theologians also suggested that Hus and his party be forbidden to preach altogether; but this the King would not approve. The rector of the University had to promise that he would announce this decision as the will of the King. The University immediately afterwards held its own meeting at which the theologians were not present, and there adopted a resolution to the effect that Wyclif's theses might be defended in their orthodox sense by members of the University.

Hus continued to preach. In fact, his defiance went further, for despite the royal prohibition against the holding of any of the forty-five articles of Wyclif, it was at this time that he either actually made public a declaration[72] (or intended to do so), in which he named seven out of the forty-five articles which he dared not to condemn, *"ne contradicerem veritati et forem mendax in conspectu domini."* But more than that: he held three public discourses in the University, sometime toward the end of July, in which he undertook to defend as wholly orthodox the articles thirteenth, fourteenth, and later the articles sixteenth, eighteenth, fifteenth, and the fourth. In defending the sixteenth article—Wyclif's thesis *"Domini temporales,"*—Hus prepared a clever mosaic from no less than six treatises and sermons of Wyclif himself.[73] In fact, about one-half of the whole defense was in Wyclif's own words. The same is true of the defense

[72] It is found in Novotný, *Korespondence*, No. 43, pp. 123-25; the form does not make it clear to whom it was addressed.
[73] Sedlák, *Studie*, II, 193-94.

of the article eighteenth, *"Nullus est dominus,"* which was almost wholly excerpted from Wyclif's *De civili dominio*.[74] This daring feat was obviously undertaken with the intention of demonstrating that Wyclif might be understood and used in a wholly acceptable sense. The defiance of Hus could not pass unnoticed: the theological faculty answered it in a series of sermons which were then presented to the Archbishop. The former Wyclifites, Stanislav and Páleč, who had at one time gone far beyond Hus in their radicalism, now rejected Wyclif altogether.

The bitter irony of the situation is found in the fact that the original cause of this struggle over indulgences which proved so disastrous to Hus no longer existed. Pope John XXIII concluded peace with King Ladislaus on October 16, 1412, although the actual warfare had ceased in the middle of June. The vindictive curia now remembered that the trial of Hus was still pending. Treating as non-existent the decision of Zabarella, which in effect pronounced the proceedings of Colonna as invalid, the Cardinal Peter degli Stephaneschi placed Hus under a stricter ban.[75] By its terms, should Hus fail to appear within the specified time at the curia, a general interdict was to be laid upon any locality in which he should reside. To this, as the last resort, Hus replied with his appeal from the papal court to Christ.[76]

In this unequal struggle against the papal curia and the royal will, Hus could not but be defeated. Before the general interdict could be pronounced, by which the whole of Prague would have been subjected to the gravest spiritual penalties, Hus decided to leave the city and thus spare its inhabitants unmerited sufferings. He left sometime in October.

Retiring into hiding, probably to the castle of Kozí near Tábor in southern Bohemia, and deprived of the possibility of preaching in his pulpit, Hus now began an extensive Czech literary activity, which was to take the place of preaching. His

[74] *Ibid.*, II, 277-301.
[75] Novotný, *Korespondence*, No. 44, pp. 125-28.
[76] *Ibid.*, No. 46, pp. 129-133.

various struggles with Zbyněk, the papal curia, and the King had now driven him into the most resolute defense of Wyclifism which he ever reached in his development. His most important, as well as beautiful, work is his *Exposition of the Faith,* intended for popular instruction. To this he conjoined his *Exposition of the Decalogue,* and *Exposition of the Lord's Prayer.* The whole trilogy was intended to expound to the common people what to believe, what to do, and how to pray. His other important Czech work, *Concerning Simony,* is a fearless and exceedingly unsparing denunciation in all its ramifications of this besetting sin of the ecclesiastical society of the time.

During this period, Hus continued to be attacked by his theological opponents in a series of virulent polemics. He replied to them in a number of treatises, the most important of which is his *De ecclesia,* which at the Council of Constance was used against him as the chief proof of his Wyclifism. It is true that Hus is here dependent upon Wyclif to a considerable degree, although Loserth's characterization of it as *in toto* the ideological property of Wyclif is grossly exaggerated, as has been already demonstrated. Hus's attitude toward Wyclif remained constant and he formulated it in one of the replies to Páleč in these words: "I confess that I adhere to the correct tenets of Master John Wyclif not because he expressed them, but because the Scriptures or infallible reason assert them. But if he asserted any heresy, I do not intend even in the least to imitate either him or any other person."[77]

Since Hus in *De ecclesia* replied to specific charges of his enemies, it is enlightening to note what it was that he rejected. In the first place, he found unacceptable the definition that the church catholic was composed of the pope as the head and the cardinals as the body.[78] To this he countered with his definition

[77] "Ego enim fateor, quod sententias ueras, quas M. Ioan Vuigleff, sacrae Theologiae professor posuit, teneo, non quia ipse dicit, sed quia dicens scriptura, uel ratio infallibilis dicit. Si autem aliquem errorem posuerit, nec ipsum quemcunque alium intendo in errore, quantumlibet modice imitari." "Responsio . . . ad scripta M. Stephani Paletz," in *Historia et monumenta,* I, 264.
[78] *The Church of John Hus,* tr. D. S. Schaff (New York, 1915), ch. VII.

of the church as the whole body of the elect, of which Christ is the head. Moreover, he rejected the assertion that all men were in duty bound to be subject in everything to the Roman bishop, and that without this submission they could not attain salvation. He replied to it:

> In this way, every Christian is expected to believe explicitly and implicitly all the truth which the Holy Spirit has put in Scripture, and in this way a man is not bound to believe the sayings of the saints which are apart from Scripture, nor should he believe papal bulls, except in so far as they speak out of Scripture, or in so far as what they say is founded in Scripture simply.[79]

Furthermore, Hus protested against his opponents' interpretation of the "power of the keys." They claimed for the church an absolute power of "binding and loosing"; Hus declared that this power was only declarative—the church only announcing God's own sovereign acts of justice and mercy in accordance with Scriptural promises. Páleč likewise charged Hus and his party that they wished "to have the holy Scripture for the sole judge," and to interpret it "according to their own heads." This charge Hus plainly branded as a lie, and affirmed that he accepted for his judges "God, the apostles, the holy doctors, or the universal church." Finally, the Páleč party asserted that the pope must[80] be acknowledged as the judge in all disputes, and that whoever should refuse to obey him should suffer death.[81] This assertion Hus repudiated as contrary to the gospel precept. These then were the matters in controversy, and made the struggle one between extreme papalism in which the Páleč party out-Bonifaced Boniface VIII, and the reform party of Hus which strove to restrain these overweening papal claims by Scriptural limitations.

The reply of Páleč, who after Stanislav's death became the chief opponent of Hus, took the form of two writings: one a long-winded treatise in the worst scholastic manner, entitled *De ecclesia,* and the other an incredibly vitriolic personal attack called *Antihus,* in which low invective and calumny vie with

[79] *Ibid.,* 71.
[80] *Ibid.,* 161, 163.
[81] *Ibid.,* 170, 171.

an obvious desire to prove Hus a heretic at all costs. From this literary sample of its author's character it is possible to derive an insight into his motives at Constance, where he was among those most zealous for the condemnation and execution of Hus. His testimony to a great extent swayed the judgment of the examining and prosecuting committee, for its members did not know Czech. He was also mainly responsible for the drawing up of the theses against Hus. Under such influences, it is no wonder that the commission gave but incredulous and sceptical hearing to the testimony of Hus himself.

In the spring of 1414, Hus decided to accept the assurances of Emperor Sigismund, granting him free passage[82] to and from the Council. To the papal court, where his legal representatives—with the exception of a short interlude—had not been permitted to present his case and had been thrown into prison, and whose judgments were regarded by Hus as unjust, he could not go. But to a general council, where he would presumably be allowed to present his case as a free man, not as one accused or already condemned, he was willing, yea eager, to go.

Hus was never a rebel against the authority of the church. For one who knew the prevailing corruption in the church's head and members as well as he did, it is astonishing that he could bring himself to believe that the General Council would permit him freely to state his position as if it were merely a case of arguing some academic proposition before a university audience. Even more astounding was his assumption that in the event that the Council were not convinced by his arguments, he would be allowed to depart in peace. Despite the explicit terms to that effect found in the safe conduct of the Emperor Sigismund, such a procedure, considering the generally prevailing notions of the conciliar theory, was unthinkable. Even though Hus could not know in detail how the Council might define its functions and powers, he must have known enough about the temper of the church not to deceive himself so grievously as to expect

[82] The text of this "safe conduct" is in Novotný, *Korespondence*, No. 88, pp. 209-10.

it to concede his demands. After all, the Council's business was the extirpation of heresy!

And yet, Hus could hardly do otherwise than to attend. The necessity was ethical: the justifiable objections which he had urged against his appearance before the papal curia were removed by the Emperor's ample promises. Even the year before he wrote in one of his sermons: "If I knew that it is God's will that I die in Rome, I would go. . . ." Hus would have been held as insincere by both his friends and his enemies had he now refused to go.

III

THE TRIAL

I

THE guileless trust reposed by Hus in the Emperor and the Council soon proved to be ill founded. It is true, as the Bishop of Constance informed Hus soon after the latter's arrival in the city, that Pope John XXIII had suspended the ban and the interdict which had been placed upon Hus, for otherwise the city of Constance would have been subject to the provisions of those sentences on account of Hus's presence there. Thus the status of Hus was somewhat puzzling, although it soon became clear in what light it was regarded. Instead of being treated as a free person, under the imperial safe conduct, who came of his own volition to present his case before the Council, he was soon treacherously seized in the Pope's residence and thrown into prison. In order to understand this high-handed treatment, we must remind ourselves that even Thomas Aquinas taught that an infidel had certain rights which ought to be respected, but a heretic had none.[1] Upon his arrival, Emperor Sigismund protested vigorously against this flagrant breach of his safe conduct. But soon prudential considerations prevailed over his honorable intentions to keep his word inviolate, and he acquiesced. The fate of Hus was sealed.

Of great importance is the fact that from the Council's point of view the whole trial of Hus was treated as a continuation of the action begun in 1410. Accordingly, it revolved around the specific attitude of Hus toward the teaching of Wyclif. For his enemies knew that a conviction of Wyclifism would eventuate in Hus's death, since Wyclif had been condemned the year before at the Roman Council. There John XXIII had condemned all the known and unknown writings of Wyclif, had ordered them burned, and had forbidden their

---

[1] *Summa theologiae*, Part II, No. 1, q. 10, art. 8.

reading.[2] Accordingly, as early as December 10 or 12, 1414, the investigating commission, appointed by the Pope, demanded from Hus, then already in prison, specific answers to the forty-five theses of Wyclif. The commission was led to believe, by the statements of Stephen Páleč and Michael de Causis, that Hus would undoubtedly profess his adherence to these articles. In fact, the commission was so certain of its ground that it had dubbed Hus a heresiarch even before the examination began.[3] It must have been a surprise, if not a shock, to the judges whose minds had been so completely predisposed to expect thorough-going Wyclifism on the part of Hus, when in a written reply he positively and unequivocally rejected thirty-three of the forty-five theses with a curt "I have not held it and do not now hold it." In regard to another three articles, he asserted that he neither affirmed nor denied them; one of these he limited to the first half of the proposition. Only in connection with nine articles did Hus reply that they might be understood in an orthodox, acceptable meaning, and explained, after properly qualifying the meaning, in what sense he would be willing to hold them.[4] But since all the forty-five articles had been already condemned, Hus by implication was guilty on account of the nine articles he held, although he did not defend the particular interpretation given them.

This was not a convenient "accommodation" on the part of Hus in an effort to save himself. That it represented his real opinions held prior to his imprisonment may be seen from his famous *"Defensio quorundam articulorum Ioannis Vvicleff,"*[5] delivered before the University late in July, 1412. There Hus defended only six articles out of the forty-five, namely the fourteenth and the fifteenth, the former asserting that those "who cease to preach or to hear the word of God . . . for fear of the

[2] H. Finke, *Acta concilii Constanciensis* (Münster, 1896), I, 162-163.
[3] Novotný, *Jan Hus*, I[2], 378.
[4] V. Flajšhans, *Obrany v Kostnici* (Praha, 1916), 10-18.
[5] *Historia et monumenta*, I, 111 ff: there exists a confusion in the numbering of these articles: In the list given C. Mirbt, *Quellen zur geschichte der Papsttums und das römischen Katholizismus* (Tübingen, 1924, 4th ed.), 229-30, the six articles referred to in this paragraph are numbered xiii, xiv, xvi, xviii, xv, iv; I follow the order of the source designated.

excommunication of men, are already excommunicate"; and the latter, "that it is lawful for any deacon or presbyter to preach the word of God without the authority of the Apostolic See, or of a Catholic bishop . . ." Besides, Hus defended the seventeenth article which asserted the right of temporal lords to deprive "habitually delinquent" clerics of temporal possessions; and the article eighteenth, declaring tithes to be pure alms; the article sixteenth, declaring that "no man is a civil lord, a bishop, or prelate, whilst he is in mortal sin" (in the sense that no one is so "worthily and justly"); and finally the fourth article, "that if a bishop or a priest be in mortal sin, he doth not ordain, consecrate the elements, nor baptize," (again modifying Wyclif's thesis by the all-saving adverb "worthily.")[6] Of Wyclif's nine articles dealing with his teaching regarding the papal office viii, ix, xxviii, xxx, xxxiii, xxxvi, xxxvii, xl, xlii), not a single one had been defended by Hus. This is significant as implying his rejection of them.[7] At about the same time, Hus wrote out an outline of his defense, in which he enumerated seven articles of the forty-five which he was willing to accept. They will be pointed out later, when all the forty-five will be treated. But it is to be noted that his denials in Constance coincided with those previously publicly avowed, except for the thirty-third article, which he "dared neither to deny nor to affirm."

Accordingly, Hus was not a blind and undiscriminating follower of Wyclif. He himself clearly formulated his attitude toward the English Reformer when he answered the accusation of one of the witnesses who deposed that he had heard Hus preach in the Bethlehem Chapel that "he would not take a chapel-full of gold in order to renounce the words and the way of Wyclif." To this Hus answered:

> Here the liar confounds a lie with truth. For I said that I would not take a chapel-full of gold in order to renounce the truth which I had learned from Wyclif's words, but I did not say, Wyclif's way. For whatever truth was propounded by Wyclif, that I accept, not because it is Wyclif's, but because it is Christ's truth.[8]

[6] This important declaration of Hus is to be found in three separate treatises in *Historia et monumenta*, I, 111-134.
[7] Kybal, *Jan Hus*, II², 24.
[8] Palacký, *Documenta*, 184.

In the final formulation of the charges, presented to Hus on June 18, 1415, one of the depositions of witnesses affirmed that "John Hus was in the said city of Prague a constant follower, friend, advocate, and defender of the errors of John Wyclif, *quondam* archheretic, and was held, named, and considered as such in the said city and the neighboring territories."

To this Hus answered point blank: "It is not true, although some of my enemies have regarded me as such."[9]

In view of the foregoing, although it is not possible to treat the matter exhaustively, at least the major specific differences in the theological concepts of the Czech and the English reformers must be considered. In this we shall follow the order of the forty-five theses, from which all the quotations are taken.[10] But it must be understood that it is not implied that these theses accurately summarize Wyclif's teaching, but only that they were so accepted by the Council and that consequently Hus was judged on their basis.

In the first place, Hus categorically repudiated the first three theses dealing with Wyclif's denial of the doctrine of transubstantiation. According to them, Wyclif affirmed "that the substance of material bread and wine doth remain in the sacrament of the altar after consecration," and "that the 'accidents' do not remain without the 'subject' in the sacrament after consecration," and that "Christ is not in the sacrament of the altar identically, truly, and really in His proper corporeal person."[11] Hus never adopted Wyclif's deductions based upon a thoroughgoing application of philosophical realism to the doctrine of transubstantiation, resulting in a concept fairly closely resembling Luther's "consubstantiation."[12] He consistently held tenets which he understood to be the orthodox dogmas of the sacraments, which he regarded, just as inconsistently as did

---

[9] *Ibid.*, 230.
[10] Flajšhans, *Obrany v Kostnici*, 10-18.
[11] The version of the twenty-four theses is taken from Workman, *John Wyclif*, II, 416, although the numbering follows Mirbt, *Quellen*, 229-30, where the text of Wyclif's forty-five theses is given in the order adopted by the Council, which differs from that given by Workman.
[12] John T. McNeill, "Some Emphases in Wyclif's Teaching," *The Journal of Religion*, VII (1927), 457.

Augustine, to be necessary to the process of sanctification. For if salvation in the last analysis depends upon predestination, sacraments can not, strictly speaking, be essential. As for the sacrament of the altar, he rejected both Wyclif's teaching of remanence and the quite current popular view that the priest "makes God." The crudeness of the popular concept against which Hus protested may be judged from his description of it in *The Exposition of the Faith:*

> From these testimonies you may see how foolishly and erroneously those priests speak who say: "We can create God or God's body whenever we desire." As if they were creators of their Creator, although all together they could not create a single fly! . . . for the Mother of God gave birth to his body but once, but a priest may create it many times and whenever he wishes.[13]

Hus held that the real presence was to be understood in a sacramental sense, and that the material bread and wine were transubstantiated into a sacramental entity. As has already been stated, in his *De corpore Christi* he had the temerity to point out by implication that the Archbishop Zbyněk's official notice forbidding the teaching of the Wyclifite doctrine of remanence erred in the opposite direction, by forbidding the use of the word "bread" as applied to the consecrated host.[14] Hus held that it was perfectly correct to speak of sacramental bread—*panis super-substantialis*—but not of material bread.

That Hus held the orthodox view of the eucharist to the end is witnessed by a small tract entitled "Concerning the most holy sacrifice of the altar," written by him in the Constance prison for the instruction, and at the request, of his jailer, Robert. In this elementary treatise he defines the sacrament as follows:

> Further one should believe that *both a good and an evil priest, holding the right faith regarding the holy sacrament and having the intention to act in accordance with the command of Christ, and repeating at the mass the words instituted by the church, transubstantiates,* that is, by the power of the words, he effects that under the form of bread there is the true body of Christ; and similarly, by his office he effects that there is the true blood of Christ. I say "by his office he effects," namely, that as a servant of Christ he effects by the words and power of Christ what Christ effects by his own

[13] Erben, *Sebrané spisy,* I, 14.
[14] Flajšhans, *Mag. Jo. Hus Opera omnia,* I², 3 ff.

words and power, transubstantiating the bread into his body and the wine into his blood.[15]

Had the fathers of the Council been disposed to credit Hus's statements regarding the sacrament of the altar, they could have found no great fault with them. The official dogma formulated by the Fourth Lateran Council just two hundred years before (1215), defined the eucharist to the effect that Christ's "body and blood are truly contained in the sacrament of the altar under the form of bread and wine, the bread being transubstantiated into body and the wine into blood, by divine power."[16]

Accordingly, Hus was in full and unequivocal agreement with the official definition that the bread and the wine are changed, transubstantiated, into the body and the blood of Christ as far as their substance is concerned, although the accidents outwardly retain the appearance of bread and wine. Hence, Hus's view was wholly orthodox. Nevertheless, he was charged in the final redaction of the articles (xxv) with repudiating the condemnation of all the articles of Wyclif and thus by inference with approving the Wyclifite articles regarding remanence. Thus the Council persisted in making him a Wyclifite in spite of himself.

The radical teaching of Wyclif, by which the sacerdotal system of the church was totally undermined, namely "that if a bishop or a priest be in mortal sin, he doth not ordain, consecrate the elements, nor baptize,"[17] was likewise rejected by Hus in that particular, absolute form. He replied to it: "I do not know where it is to be found. It is correct in the sense, as the saints assert, that (such a cleric) does not ordain, transubstantiate, and consecrate worthily; but otherwise, even the worst priest does so, for God performs it through him."[18] This fully agrees with his previously expressed statements, made even during the heat of his controversy with the Páleč party. In 1413 he wrote in one of his sermons:

15 *Sebrané spisy*, V, 230-231.
16 Mirbt, *Quellen*, 179.
17 *Ibid.*, 229.
18 Flajšhans, *Obrany*, 10.

It may be and often is that although the bishop is wicked, yet he who with good intention and order piously receives consecration from him, receives a gift of the Holy Spirit. Not from the bishop, but from a higher one than he, Christ, who consecrates his faithful. Likewise when a wicked priest baptizes or grants absolution, a man of good intentions receives the Holy Spirit from Christ through the act of the wicked priest.[19]

Thus Hus held to the orthodox Catholic view, asserted by Augustine in his struggle with the Donatists, that the validity of the sacraments does not depend upon the personal character of the officiating priest. But in his reforming zeal he also stressed the view that a bishop or a priest in mortal sin does not perform his functions worthily, and hence ministers to his own condemnation.[20] Being an unworthy prelate or priest, he is in reality not a true member of the church, and hence not a true prelate or priest. Nevertheless, his acts are not thereby invalidated. It was the adverb "worthily" which made all the difference between the position of Wyclif and Hus. And by ignoring this important modification, the Council persisted in misjudging Hus's true view. As against Hus, Stephen Páleč claimed that an evil priest not only administers valid sacraments, but administers them worthily, and hence is a worthy servant of the church.[21]

In regard to the fifth article, that "It hath no foundation in the Gospel that Christ did ordain the Mass," Hus replied: "I do not know where it is recorded. It is correct in the sense that Christ did not appoint the service of the mass in the Gospels, but he gave the priests the possibility of celebrating it." As to the sixth article, "that God ought to obey the devil," Hus curtly and categorically answered: "It is false." The seventh article read: "If a man be duly contrite, all outward confession is for him superfluous and unnecessary." This Hus countered by: "I do not know where it is recorded. I do not and never have held it, but I read the contrary in the Gospel: 'Jesus was descending from the mountain, . . . ' "

[19] "Postil," Sebrané spisy, I, 140.
[20] As already mentioned, this was the sense in which Hus treated the article in 1412: "Patet, quia si iam dictis non est digne Episcopus uel Sacerdos, tunc nec digne ordinat, conficit, uel baptisat." "De decimis," in Historia et monumenta, I, 134.
[21] Kybal, Jan Hus, II², 213.

A great deal of emphasis has been placed upon Hus's anti-papalism, which has been commonly identified with that of Wyclif. It is perfectly true that in comparison with the rest of the relatively moderate, conservative tenets of Hus, his views of the office of the papacy were radical. But it must be borne in mind that Hus protested primarily against the excesses of the papalist theory, the ultramontanism and papal infallibilism of the time.

> They likewise blaspheme who assert that the pope cannot err, and that men should obey him in all things, and that he can send whomsoever he wishes to heaven or to hell. For such power belongs to God alone. They likewise blaspheme who say that the pope is an earthly god, who may do whatever he pleases on earth, and who may rule all men as he pleases; and those who say that he may set up another law against God's law or rightfully issue commands which are contrary to those of the holy apostles. They likewise say that no one on earth should speak against him, no matter what he does.[22]

It was such extravagant papalism that Hus opposed.

But, for that matter, the whole age—the age of the Great Schism—was necessarily critical of the papacy. In fact, the Council of Constance was rigorous with Hus in order to avoid being charged with anti-papalism and doctrinal laxity. For the conciliar principle—that the general council is superior to the pope—was essentially anti-papal. It is highly significant that out of the final thirty articles on the basis of which Hus was condemned in the fifteenth session of the Council on July 6, 1415, twenty-two deal with theses concerning the church and the papal office. Nevertheless, Hus, as usual, kept clear of Wyclif's overstatements and extremism. He denied the eighth article of the forty-five theses, which stated that "if the pope, according to the divine foreknowledge, be an evil man, and consequently a member of the devil, he hath no power over the faithful of Christ given to him by any, unless, peradventure, by the emperor." He likewise rejected the next thesis: "That after Urban VI none other is to be received as pope, but that Christendom ought to live after the manner of the Greeks under its own laws."[23] The comment of Hus to the first proposition was:

22 "Concerning Simony," in Erben, *Spisy*, I, 392.
23 Workman, *John Wyclif*, II, 416.

"I do not and never have held it, but affirm that even the worst pope has the power, by virtue of his office, through which God acts, according to Matthew XXIII: 'On the seats of Moses, etc.'" To the ninth article he replied: "I have never held it and do not now hold it, since I have acknowledged as popes Boniface, Innocent, Gregory, Alexander, and the present pope, John XXIII."[24] Like Wyclif, Hus argued that the only real title to the papal office is worthiness of character. "Hence any pope is called apostolic so far as he teaches the doctrine of the apostles and follows them in works. But, if he puts the teaching of the apostles aside, teaching in word and works what is contrary, then he is properly called pseudo-apostolic or an apostate."[25] "If his (the pope's) life be contrary to the life of Jesus Christ, he is Christ's adversary, even though he hold the place and office of Christ." "Accordingly, even the pope is a sinful man, particularly venially, but may sin mortally. If he lives well to the end, he shall be saved; but if evilly, he shall be damned."[26] But unlike Wyclif, Hus made an important distinction between the papal office and the pope's character. He asserted that no matter how unworthy as to character a pope might be, he was still legally a pope as far as his office was concerned, and as such obedience was due him in all things lawful. But unless he be among the predestinate, he did not truly and worthily hold his office, was not truly "a successor of Peter," for he was not in reality even a member of the true church—that is the company of the predestinate—despite the fact that he might hold the highest office in the Roman church. Hus cited the example of fifteen popes whom he regarded as unworthy of their office,[27] although he did not deny the validity of their jurisdiction as far as their office was concerned. Nevertheless, despite Hus's assertions to the contrary, the unmodified Wyclifite version (although not in the identical words of theses viii and ix, for it rather follows art. xxxvii) was inserted into

---

[24] Flajšhans, *Obrany*, 11.
[25] D. S. Schaff, ed., *John Hus, The Church* (New York, 1915), 197.
[26] "Exposition of the Faith," in Erben, *Spisy*, I, 8,9.
[27] Schaff, *The Church*, 178-81.

the final charges against him (arts. xii and xiii), and he was condemned to death for what he had never taught. The most curious part of the matter is that this same Council deposed three popes. It declared one of them, John XXIII, "to be guilty of simony and a waster of the goods of the church both in things spiritual and temporal," and described his character "as a scandal to all Christendom."[28]

Furthermore, the thirty-seventh article affirmed that "the Roman church is the synagogue of Satan, and the pope is not the immediate and nearest vicar of Christ and the apostles." To this Hus replied: "I have never held it and do not now hold it, for I have written the contrary in the treatise *De ecclesia*." Similarly, the fortieth article asserted that "the election of the pope by the cardinals was instituted by the devil." Hus catagorically repudiated it.

This matter is closely connected with the concept of the church held by Hus, which is very similar to that of Wyclif, although ultimately both concepts are essentially Augustinian. Against his opponents, Stanislav of Znojmo and Stephen Páleč, who had put forth the exaggerated thesis, condemned by implication by the Council of Constance, that the pope is the head of the church and the cardinals its body,[29] Hus defined the true church as the totality of the predestinate. This, then, was the true, universal, catholic church, of which Christ alone was the head, while the predestinate formed its body. The church which existed at the time, the church militant, was composed of both the predestinate and the foreknown—sheep and goats, saints and sinners. Of this church militant the Roman church was part, and it was of this latter church that the pope was the head —either worthily or otherwise. The Council refused to allow the distinctions made by Hus, and condemned him (arts. i, iii, v, vii, x, xi, xii, xxviii) as if he had denied the authority, or the very existence, of the Roman church—and consequently the

[28] John P. McGowan, *Pierre d'Ailly and the Council of Constance* (Washington, 1936), 65.
[29] "Responsio ad scripta Magistri Stanislai de Znoyma, doct. Theologiae," in *Historia et monumenta*, I, 266.

authority of the Council which claimed to represent that church.

The distinction made by Hus between the true, universal church—the totality of the predestinate—and the Roman church, did not imply that he refused to acknowledge the authority of the Roman church or repudiated obedience to it. As he expressed the matter in *De ecclesia,* "obedience should be rendered the pope and cardinals so long as they teach the truth according to God's law." "But if . . . popes and cardinals charge or admonish anything besides the truth, even though the whole Roman curia is on their side, the faithful is not to obey when he knows the truth."[30] In his letter to John XXIII dated September 1, 1411, Hus had asserted his obedience in clear and unmistakable terms.[31]

Knowing the reforming zeal of Hus, and his invectives against the money-grubbing, avaricious clergy and monks, it is instructive to observe the moderate position taken by him in regard to Wyclif's radical demand of "apostolic poverty." The tenth article of the forty-five theses asserted that "it is contrary to Holy Scriptures that ecclesiastical persons should have temporal possessions." Hus rejected it, saying: "I have never held it and do not now hold it, but adhere in this matter to the opinion of St. Augustine, Jerome, Gregory, and other saints." The thirty-second article piled Pelion on Ossa by affirming that "To enrich clergy is against the rule of Christ." Hus responded: "I have never held it and do not now hold it, for the clergy may hold possessions properly, if they do not abuse them." Furthermore, the thirty-third article asserted: "Pope Sylvester and Emperor Constantine erred in endowing the church." Hus returned a cautious answer, saying: "I dare neither to affirm nor to deny it, for both could have sinned venially, the latter in giving and the former in receiving." The thirty-sixth article again attacked the riches of the pope by asserting: "The pope with all his clergy possessing property, are heretics because they own property—as well as all who agree with them, that is, the

[30] Schaff, *The Church,* 168.
[31] Novotný, *Korespondence,* No. 31, p. 95.

temporal lords and other laymen." Again, Hus unequivocally countered with an approach to a sarcastic repartee: "I have never held it and do not now hold it, for I myself possess property."

There is similarly an important difference between Hus and Wyclif in the matter of property holding in general. The fifteenth article stated that "No man is a civil lord, a bishop, or prelate, whilst he is in mortal sin." To this Hus replied: "According to the opinion of St. Augustine, Jerome, Ambrose, Gregory, Chrysostom, Remigius, and Gratian, this sentence possesses a correct sense, that is, that no one is such worthily, although he is such according to his office." Thus a lord—civil or ecclesiastical—sinning mortally retained his office and possessions before men, but before God he was not entitled to them. This thesis had been plainly stated as early as 1412.[32] In his last reply on June 18, 1415, Hus reiterated his affirmation in this properly modified form. Nevertheless, the unmodified thesis was retained in the final redaction of the charges (art. xxx),[33] and Hus was condemned on the basis of this tenet which he had never held.

Very offensive to the prelates was the sixteenth article, affirming that "temporal lords may at will withdraw their temporal goods from ecclesiastics habitually delinquent." In this very delicate matter, a modification or softening of Hus's earlier opinion may be discerned: in 1412 he had affirmed Wyclif's thesis unequivocally.[34] In his exceedingly earnest and even polemical treatise, *Concerning Simony,* completed early in 1413, he had again advocated secular supervision over the clergy as far as an unworthy use of their endowments was concerned. Simony should be suppressed, by right and in the first place, by the pope. But alas! "it would indeed be a mighty miracle if such a pope should now appear; I am certain that his apostles would not let him live long!"[35] Failing the papacy, secular

---

[32] Novotný, *Korespondence,* No. 43, pp. 124-25; also *Historia et monumenta,* I, 134: "Nullus est digne et iuste ciuilis Dominus, dum est in peccato mortali."
[33] Mirbt, *Quellen,* 231.
[34] Novotný, *Korespondence,* No. 43.
[35] *Sebrané spisy,* V, 200-201.

princes and lords should uproot the evil. The most effective method is the confiscation of superfluous temporalities, and restriction of the income of the clergy to the necessities of living. "For as fire ever burns and consumes as long as there is anything to consume, so the devil's fire ever burns in the entire world into which it is cast as long as it has something to feed on." In the third place, the church authorities should withhold benefices from simoniac clerics. Hus had defended the proposals by citing examples from the Old and the New Testaments. No wonder that such radical remedies seemed to the anti-reformists as worse than the disease! But at Constance Hus temporized, saying: "I neither affirm nor deny it, for it may possess a correct meaning." On this point Hus might have honestly changed his mind. At any rate, it need not be interpreted as impugning the character of Hus, for after all he did not deny the thesis!

As for the functions and prerogatives of the clergy and the prelates, the eleventh thesis asserted as Wyclif's teaching that "No prelate ought to excommunicate any man except he first know him to be excommunicated by God; and he who doth so excommunicate is thereby himself a heretic or excommunicated." Hus replied discriminatingly, asserting that "The first part of the thesis seems correct, for no prelate should excommunicate anyone except for a mortal sin, as is asserted in the canon law."

The twelfth article asserted: "A bishop excommunicating a cleric who hath appealed to the king or to the council of the realm in so doing is a traitor to God, the king, and the realm." Hus categorically repudiated the assertion: "I have never held it, do not now hold it, and do not believe that it is correct."

To the following thesis, "They who cease to preach or to hear the word of God or the preached gospel, for fear of the excommunication of men, are already excommunicate, and in the day of judgment shall be held traitors to God," Hus assented with qualifications. Pointing out that he had adhered to the conciliar principle as affirmed by the Council of Pisa sooner than the Archbishop Zbyněk did, Hus replied diplomatically: "This might possess a correct meaning. For it happened to me that on account of my renunciation of obedience to Gregory, the Archbishop of Prague forbade me to preach and to conduct services. But I continued to preach, and disregarded his excommunication."

The fourteenth thesis affirmed: "It is lawful for any deacon or presbyter to preach the word of God without the authority of the Apostolic See or of a Catholic bishop." Hus replied saying: "This may possess a correct meaning; namely, that in times of great need it may be permitted that a deacon or priest preach without any special authorization."

As for the validity of ecclesiastical functions and regulations, the eighteenth article asserted that "tithes are pure alms, and that parishioners may, on account of the sins of their prelates, detain them and bestow them on others at pleasure." Hus gave in this instance a somewhat evasive answer, saying: "As for the first part, I dare neither to deny nor to affirm it; but I deny the second part." But there can be no doubt that previously Hus unequivocally called tithes alms. In his *Postil* of 1413 he wrote in one of the sermons:

> And although they rejected (the article) that tithes are truly alms, still since they live on tithes, they are almoners, although they do not wish to be called so; for they did not secure them (the tithes) by inheritance, nor did they win them in a game of dice, unless some bought the benefice from the pope or someone else and thus came by it in such a way. Nevertheless, tithes are alms given for the sake of souls for God's praise. Accordingly, they are called "the soul-pay" (*zádušní*). Moreover, when anyone wishes to withhold the tithes, they complain, lament, cry, and preach that they are being deprived and stripped of their poor "soul-pay!" But when no one interferes, then they call it rule! The devil's lords! When were they called to earthly rule by Christ?[36]

The seventeenth article affirmed that "the common people may at will correct delinquent lords." Hus answered that "If the term 'correct' is to be understood as 'kindly counsel,' according to Matthew VIII: 'If a brother sin, etc.,' then it may possess a correct meaning."

The bellicose fulminations and tirades of Wyclif denouncing the laziness and cupidity of the monks and friars, are well

[36] *Ibid.*, VI, 77-78.

known. Quite a number of articles of the forty-five theses deal
with this matter. Only a few samples are here cited as illustra-
tions of this class of charges. Thus the thirty-fourth article
states that "all members of the mendicant orders are heretics and
those who give them alms are excommunicated." To this Hus
replied: "I have never held it and do not hold it, for I trust
that they are good Christians, and I myself often gave them
alms and concerned myself about contributions to them." The
thirty-fifth article asserts: "Whoever enters religious life or
an order, is thereby disabled to observe the commandments of
God; consequently he cannot enter the kingdom of heaven, unless he abandon them." There is a note of mistrust of the
monastic vocation in Hus's reply: "I have never held it nor do
I hold it now, although for some it is perhaps more difficult
to keep the rules than to observe the general law of Christ."
The forty-fourth article goes so far as to affirm: "Augustine,
Benedict, and Bernard are damned unless they repented on
account of possessing property and of having founded orders
and having joined them; accordingly, from the pope to the least
monk, all are heretics." This was easy for Hus to refute; he
said, "I have never held it nor do I hold it now: indeed, I regard
St. Augustine especially as a great and holy doctor of the
church."

In addition to these tenets enumerated in the forty-five
theses, Hus differed from Wyclif even in the all-important matter of the authority of the Scriptures. The latter held them to
be the sole and absolute rule in matters of faith and conduct.
Accordingly, he rejected all tradition, and adhered to the pa-
tristic teaching only so far as it was in accordance with the
Scriptures. Thus since God's commands were explained *"suf-
ficientissime"* in the holy Scriptures, men owed obedience to
them alone.[37] Consequently, all human ordinances, civil and ecclesiastical, not contained in the *"lex ewangelica"* are superfluous
and wicked.[38]

[37] *De civili dominio,* I, ch. 33, p. 379.
[38] *Ibid.,* 399.

Again Hus had no part in the radicalism of Wyclif. Páleč, in his *Antihus,* charged him with the rejection of all ecclesiastical authority on the ground that Hus held to the Wyclifite tenet of *"sola Scriptura."* From this he concluded that Hus rejected everything which was not found in the Scriptures. On the other hand Páleč affirmed that the authority of the Roman curia was absolute, and *all* its pronouncements were in conformity with the Scriptures.[39] This charge was repeated in his *Tractatus gloriosus,* in which Hus was accused of being of the "Armenian sect" which was said to adhere only to the Scriptures and to reject all other authority.

Hus differed from Wyclif, in the first place, in distinguishing between the degrees of inspiration of the Old and New Testaments, in favor of the latter. Furthermore, he summarily denied Páleč's accusation. He stated that he acknowledged as his judges beside the Scriptures, also "God, the apostles, the holy doctors of the church, and the catholic church."[40] Thus Hus accepted tradition as the secondary source of dogmatic and canonical authority, but definitely subordinated it to the Scriptures. Specifically, Hus acknowledged the authority of the apostolic tradition, of the creeds, the writings of the doctors of the church, particularly of Ambrose, Jerome, Augustine, Gregory the Great, Athanasius, Basil the Great, Gregory Nazianzen, and John Chrysostom. Besides these, he often quoted such theologians of repute as Bernard of Clairvaux, Anselm, Thomas Aquinas, and Peter Lombard. Moreover, Hus accepted as authoritative the decisions of general councils. He was ready to submit to the decision of the Council of Constance, and came to attend its meeting voluntarily.[41]

On the other hand, Hus denied that the pope, or anyone else, had the right to define or order anything without, or contrary to, the Scriptural warrant, as for instance in the case of the papal indulgence bull. In such a case every Christian, layman or cleric, had the right, nay even the duty, to disobey

[39] Kybal, *Jan Hus,* II[1], 40, 49.
[40] *Ibid.,* II[2], 60 ff.
[41] *Ibid.,* II[2], 61-71.

the order on the ground that God must be obeyed rather than man. Likewise, in the matter of Wyclif's rejection of all civil and ecclesiastical bans as "superfluous," Hus adhered to the sober and moderate middle ground. He recognized the validity of civil and ecclesiastical jurisdiction, provided it were not in conflict with, or directly contrary to, the Scriptural precepts.[42]

To present every step of the trial in detail would be tedious. That the various charges against Hus, assembled for the most part by his known enemies such as Stephen Páleč and Michael de Causis, were often baseless lies or statements wrenched and distorted from their original meaning, may be gathered from the fact that the successive commissions eliminated a great many of such accusations from the later lists. After the flight of Pope John XXIII from Constance, following his deposition on May 29, the trial of Hus entered upon a new phase, for the papal commission had thereby lost its jurisdiction. Had the Emperor wished, he could now have freed Hus. But instead, he turned him over to the Council, which appointed its own commission.

The ultimate formulation of the charges comprised twenty-nine theses,[43] which were based largely on the writings of Hus, especially his *De ecclesia,* and the polemical works against Stephen Páleč and Stanislav. Besides, there were sixteen other charges compiled largely by Michael de Causis from the testimonies of various witnesses,[44] most of which had been disproved by Hus long before. Páleč had excerpted thirty-four such charges from *De ecclesia,* but the commission reduced these to eleven, although it added twenty-eight other theses considered heretical. The forty-five theses of Wyclif do not figure prominently among these last charges, although some few, even those which Hus had rejected or had properly delimited as to their meaning at the very beginning of the investigation, were retained among them. Such were the twentieth article, which corresponds essentially to the eighth article of the forty-five theses, and the thirtieth article, which is identical with the fifteenth article of

[42] *Ibid.*, II[1], 368.
[43] The text given in Mirbt, *Quellen,* 230-31.
[44] Palacký, *Documenta,* 225-234.

the latter. There are, of course, many others reminiscent of Wyclif's articles. Since Wyclif and his forty-five theses, as well as
two hundred and sixty additional ones, had been solemnly condemned in the session of May 4, the two articles with which Hus
was charged were *ipso facto* incriminating—except that he did
not really hold them in the sense in which they had been condemned. Hus added to these charges explanatory remarks which,
had the commission been willing to consider them, would have
materially changed their meaning. Thirteen of the sixteen of
these accusations were based upon "testimonies of witnesses."
Hus summarily rejected them with a curt, "It is not true." Of the
remaining three, he acknowledged only one as wholly true—
the "crime" of appealing to Pope Alexander! When these final
charges, expanded to thirty by the division of the article twenty
into two separate articles,[45] had been read to him in the session
of the Council on the very day of the execution—July 6—Hus
again wished to explain which ones he repudiated and in what
sense he held the others. But he was not permitted to speak.
Both the president, Cardinal d'Ailly, and the reader, Cardinal
Zabarella, ordered him to keep silent.

The tragic character of the trial cannot be understood without a clear realization of the contradictory conception, held by
Hus and the Council, of the nature of the trial. Hus agreed to
go to the Council not as one accused, but as a free Christian
desiring to present his views before the assembled representatives of the Christian church in order to receive correction on
the basis of the Scriptures, if he had erred in anything. In this
sense Hus was willing, and repeatedly affirmed his willingness,
not to defend any view stubbornly, but to abandon every position
proved contrary to the Scriptures. Long before, he had defined
heresy as an "erroneous doctrine contrary to the holy Scriptures
and stubbornly defended."[46] To the last he pleaded with the
commission and the Council to be shown wherein the articles
which he acknowledged as his own were contrary to the Scrip-

[45] Sedlák, *Studie*, II, 27-34.
[46] "Concerning Simony," in *Sebrané spisy*, V, 140.

tures. The Council, on the other hand, never dreamed of arguing with an accused heretic—for such Hus was held to be—for the purpose of convincing him of his error. It claimed to be the supreme tribunal in the Christian church, and its judgments were binding on all members of the church, from the popes to the least layman.[47] It was a special concession granted to Hus that he had been allowed public hearings at all; a concession grudgingly made to Emperor Sigismund, who on his part then ceased pressing the claims of his "safe conduct" which he had granted to Hus. That the leaders of the Council never really meant to live up to their promise to grant the Czech Reformer a free hearing is evident from the fact that even on the first of these occasions the sentence had been drawn up even before the hearing began.

Nothing can better illustrate this fundamental difference between the points of view of the Council and Hus than the record of the most reliable of the eye-witnesses of the trial, a devoted adherent of the Czech Reformer, Peter of Mladoňovic. He describes one of the scenes at the Council after a public hearing given to Hus, when Cardinal d'Ailly attempted by earnest exhortation to secure Hus's recantation:

'Master John! Behold, you have two paths before you, from which you may choose one: either that you submit completely and altogether to the mercy and into the hands of the Council, that whatever disposition the Council should make of you, therewith you rest satisfied. The Council, from respect of the Roman King here present, and of his brother the King of Bohemia, and for your own good, shall deal kindly and lovingly with you. Or if you still desire to hold and defend some of the previously mentioned theses, and wish for another hearing, it shall be granted you. But consider that there are present here famous and brilliant men, doctors and masters, who have such strong arguments against your theses that it must be feared lest you become entangled in still greater errors if you should hold and defend these theses. I advise you, and do not speak as a judge.' And others added: 'Indeed, Master John, it were better for you to submit yourself completely to the mercy of the Council, as the Lord Cardinal says, and to hold nothing stubbornly.'

And the master bending his head, replied with humility: 'Most reverend fathers! I came here freely not that I should stubbornly defend any views,

[47] "Haec sancta synodus Constantiensis . . . primo declarat, quod . . . cui quilibet, cuiuscunque status vel dignitatis, etiamsi papalis existat, obedire tenetur in his, quae pertinent ad fidem et extirpationem schismatis et reformationem ecclesiae in capite et membris." Mirbt, *Quellen*, 228.

but that if I had presented some view not quite properly or faultily, I might submit humbly to the instruction of the Council. But I pray for God's sake that I be granted hearing for the exposition of my meaning and of the writings of holy doctors regarding the theses which are laid to my charge. And if my proofs and those of the writings should prove insufficient, I am willing to submit humbly to the Council.'

Thereupon instantly many shouted, saying: 'Behold, he speaks with reservations and stubbornly. He is willing to submit to the instruction of the Council, but not its correction and decision.'

He then answered: 'Yes, to the instruction, correction, and decision of the Council I am willing to submit. God is my witness that I speak sincerely, not with reservations.'

Thereupon the Cardinal of Cambrai said to him: 'Master John! Since you are willing to throw yourself on the mercy of the Council and to submit to its instruction, then know that the instruction to you by at least sixty doctors (of whom some have already left and those from Paris have just come), without any demur and by the command and order of the Council, is as follows: that, first of all, you humbly acknowledge the error of those theses which you have hitherto held; secondly, that you recant those theses, and swear that you shall never again hold, preach, or teach them; third, that you publicly renounce and reject those theses; and fourth that you expound, profess, and teach the opposite of what you have held, written, and preached (as was here proved against you).'

Then Master John, among many other things, discussed and brought out here and there, said: 'Most reverent father! I am ready humbly to obey the Council and to receive instruction. But I implore for God's sake that you do not lay before me traps of damnation, that I be not forced to lie, and to recant those theses about which—God and my conscience are my witnesses—nothing is known to me. The witnesses bear testimony against me about matters that have never entered my mind, especially that after the consecration material bread remains in the sacrament of the altar. Those, however, of which I know and which I have incorporated in my books, I am willing—after receiving instruction to the contrary—humbly to recant. But if I should recant all the theses charged against me, of which many, God knows, are falsely ascribed to me, I should prepare for myself by lying a trap of damnation. For 'to recant,' as I remember having read in the *Catholicon*, is to renounce an error previously held. But since many of the theses ascribed to me which I have never held and which have never even entered my mind, it seems to be against my conscience that I should recant them and to lie.'[48]

It is in the light of this understanding that the conduct of Hus must be viewed. Although the Council was governed by a policy of expediency, as may be seen from the astonishing fact that the fourteenth session was convoked in the name of Pope Gregory XII who had been deposed by the Council of

[48] Peter of Mladoňovic, "Relatio de Mag. Joannis Hus causa" (Palacký, *Documenta*), 308-309.

Pisa, because this was one of the conditions stipulated by Gregory as the *sine quâ non* of his abdication, and the Council accepted it despite the fact that it thereby logically and legally undermined its own bases of authority, yet in the case of Hus the Council felt that its authority must be asserted. Nevertheless, on its part, it in the end went so far as to offer Hus a compromise, a delimited form of recantation. Hus was to renounce on oath such theses as had been selected from his books, and such portions of the testimonies of the witnesses, as he had acknowledged to be accurately reported. As for the testimony of the witnesses the truth of which he had denied, he was to swear that he did not hold them and never would.[49] But even this extreme concession was not acceptable to Hus, who in response referred to the final declaration of his principles offered to the representatives of the Council on July 1. This brief declaration is of the greatest importance for the comprehension of the issues involved, and is as follows:

I, John Hus, in hope a priest of Jesus Christ, fearing to offend God and to commit perjury, am not willing to abjure all or any of the theses which were brought against me in the testimonies of the false witnesses. For as God is my witness, I have never preached them, nor asserted them, nor defended them, as they said that I had defended, preached, and asserted them.

Furthermore, regarding the articles taken from my books, at least those correctly abstracted, I say that whichever of them contains an incorrect meaning, that I reject. But fearing to offend against the truth, and to speak against the statements of saints, I am not willing to abjure any of them. And if it were possible that my voice might be heard throughout the world, as every lie and every sin of mine shall be revealed at the day of judgment, most gladly would I recant every falsehood and every error before all the world which I taught, imagined, or expressed.

This I say and write freely and voluntarily.

Written by my own hand on the first day of July.[50]

Accordingly, Hus could not recant what he had never held, for to him "recantation" implied the previous holding of such views. On the other hand, he could not recant the theses which had been taken from his books, even those he had acknowledged to have been correctly formulated, unless he were convinced by the commission with proofs from the Scriptures that they

[49] Novotný, *Jan Hus*, II, 452.
[50] Novotný, *Korespondence*, No. 162, p. 333.

6

were erroneous. In that case he was willing gladly to recant them. Without such a proof of their erroneous nature, to recant involved a betrayal of the truth. His conscience was too sensitive to permit him to do it. He who had written: "Therefore, O faithful Christian, search for truth, hear truth, learn truth, love truth, speak the truth, hold the truth till death,"[51] could not now himself deny the truth in order to save his life. In other words, the Council insisted on judging what was wrong as it seemed proper to it, and then demanded that Hus submit unconditionally to this judgment, whether or not he were convinced of its correctness. From the Council's premises, that is, as being the highest tribunal in Christendom, this position was justifiable; granting the presuppositions of Hus, it follows that he could not act otherwise than he did unless he betrayed his convictions. That is the tragedy of the trial of Hus.

Consequently, nothing remained for the Council to do but to condemn Hus to death as an incorrigible heretic.

II

It is sufficiently clear from the foregoing that even in the most important tenets of Wyclif, Hus differed essentially from the latter, and always in the direction of moderation and conservatism. We are, accordingly, now in a position to give an answer to the question raised at the beginning of this study as to the degree of dependence of Hus upon Wyclif. It is evident that the Council's condemnation of Hus as a Wyclifite did not rest upon a foundation of verified and proved facts; the majority of the charges were repudiated by Hus as either wholly contrary to his beliefs and tenets, or as couched in a garbled form which distorted his meaning. Since in accordance with the usages of the time a man accused of heresy was not held innocent until he was proved guilty, and his self-defense was discounted in advance as unworthy of credence, the trial of Hus was not conducted in accordance with the fair and equitable rules which we moderns expect in connection with a process of law. As this investigation has shown, Hus was not guilty of holding the

[51] "Exposition of the Faith," in Erben, *Spisy*, I, 7.

great majority of charges upon which he was condemned to death. Accordingly, he was executed unjustly.

But if the Council put Hus to death as a heretic, and if all the Wyclifite charges ascribed to him could not be sustained had Hus received what in our modern notion passes for a fair trial, then it follows that those historians who concur with the Council in regarding Hus as a thoroughgoing Wyclifite err in this judgment. Hus may in reality be described as a medieval scholastic of the "leftist" orientation, as Kybal had characterized him,[52] or still better, as the best representative of the Czech reform movement. That is why his ideas agree essentially with those of his reformist predecessors, even though he goes beyond them, and despite the fact that he often expresses them in the language of Wyclif. For the same reason, Hus's chief interest lay in moral reform, rather than in ecclesiastical revolt or in theological speculation. Accordingly, his essential characteristics are not of the Wyclifite, but of the native, reform movement.

Nevertheless, if the Council condemned Hus for many "heresies" he did not actually hold, it must be admitted that it sensed the direction which the consequences of the premises of Hus would take. For that reason, it would be a grave mistake to let the matter rest with the judgment expressed above; for there are certain elements in the presuppositions and convictions of Hus which logically and inevitably lead to the subversion of the very foundations of the Roman Catholic ecclesiastical structure and doctrine. It would be an error to regard Hus merely as a medieval scholastic. There are two sides to him, which could be loosely designated as Catholic and Protestant, as was the case with Augustine. There were elements implicit in Hus's teaching which the Reformation made explicit. These elements were characteristic of the principles of the Protestant Reformation. Hus was doubtless quite unconscious of the ultimate conclusions which must be in course of time inevitably drawn from his principles. For that matter, the church, too, was not fully aware of the full scope of their implications. The

[52] Kybal, *Jan Hus*, II[1], 37.

Council of Trent was clear as to the consequences of these views, and defined its positions accordingly.

But to affirm that these views of Hus contributed to the principles of the Reformation does not imply the fallacious doctrine of *"post hoc, ergo propter hoc."* Nothing would be more misleading than to affirm that Luther received his ideas from Hus, who in turn had derived them from Wyclif. The familiar representation of the torch being passed on from Wyclif, through Hus, to Luther, makes a pretty picture, but is hardly to be taken as a strictly critical portrayal of historical truth. Moreover, Luther went considerably beyond Hus in his rejection of the orthodox Catholic system of doctrine. All that is here attempted is to point out which of the tenets of Hus tended, under the stress of later developments, to contribute to the process of differentiation which in the end resulted in that schism within western Christendom known as the Reformation.

What, then, were the implicit elements in the tenets of Hus which, in their explicit, developed form, culminated in, and contributed to, the Protestant Reformation? First of all, the biblicism of Hus clearly manifested this tendency. As has already been pointed out, Hus did not hold the doctrine of *"sola Scriptura,"* but when the inevitable conflict between the authority of the church and the Scriptures flared up, Hus's view was unmistakably on the side of the latter. This may be seen from the fact that the Taborites—admittedly an extreme group among the Hussites—and the Unity of Czech Brethren, acknowledged the Scriptures as the sole rule of faith and practice. On the other hand, the Utraquists did not go beyond Hus in this matter. Nevertheless, the step which Hus himself refused to take, was in the end taken by others who were to a considerable degree under the influence of Hussitism.

His definition of the church as the totality of the predestinate was contrary to the tendency which ultimately led to the affirmation of papal infallibility. The Protestant Reformation, therefore, found support in Hus for its definition of the church and its rejection of the whole system of papalism. If one's salvation ultimately rested upon the divine predestination—the inscrutable and sovereign will of God, as both Luther and Calvin asserted—the visible church ceased to be central in the scheme of salvation.

The predestinarian tenet of Hus likewise logically led to the undermining of the sacramental and sacerdotal systems of the Roman church. Since salvation ultimately derived from the fact of divine election, the whole system of sacraments and all other external aids to salvation were not fundamental or primary, as the later Reformers, with varying degrees of consistency, brought out in their teachings. Although this was not clearly realized by Hus himself, yet in the end the implication of his position became apparent.

Hus's insistence that no man should obey his ecclesiastical superior, even the pope, unless his commands be in conformity with the Scriptures, was in line with the later Protestant idea of the priesthood of all believers. The startling insistence on the use of reason foreshadowed the Age of Reason, and made for Protestant individualism which was essentially destructive of ecclesiastical authority. Hus's own noble protest against the blind submission of one's conscience to the dictates of ecclesiastical authority clearly implied the assumption of essential freedom of conscience which in his case took the form of the affirmation that one must obey God rather than man. His insistence at the Council that he could not submit to its fiat unless he be first convinced of its truth by proofs from the Scriptures or arguments from reason, forecast the implicit principles of the Reformation and even went beyond them. At any rate, such a position clearly differentiated him from all the previous medievalists, and linked him with modern men. This feature of Hus's religious view is of the very essence of the modern religious conception, for it affirmed that external authority has no place in the realm of truth. Life of the spirit is essentially free.

But above all, it was the heroic example and the moral earnestness of the Czech Reformer which constitute his most potent influence. The Czech Reformation always stressed the quality of life, ethical conduct, rather than abstract thought. Hus also stressed conscience, rather than intellect. It was his moral courage, enabling him to stand alone against the judgment of the supreme tribunal of the Church, which marked him as great. It was his devoted search for truth, his stern moral emphasis, his zeal for reform, his sterling character, and his insistence upon personal responsibility in matters of religion which secured for him the influence which he has enjoyed ever since.

INDEX

Alexander IV, Pope, 6
Alexander V, Pope, 28, 34, 39, 61, 70
Ambrose, St., 64, 68
Anselm, 68
Antihus of Páleč, 50, 68
Aristotle, 35
Athanasius, 68
Augustine, St., 12-14, 20, 24, 63-64, 67-68, 75.

Bacon, Francis, 13
Bartoš, F. M., 1, 15
Basil the Great, 68
Bede, Venerable, 13
Benedict of Nursia, 67
Bernard of Clairvaux, 12, 67-68
Bethlehem Chapel, 6-7, 25, 31, 35-36, 39, 46, 55
Blackfriars' Synod of 1382, 21
Bohemia, 18, 39, 43, 48
Boniface VIII, Pope, 50
Bradwardine, Archbishop, 20
de Brancaiis, Cardinal, 41
Bratislava, 41

Calvin, John, 77
Chesterton, Gilbert K., 12
Chrysostom, John, 12, 64, 68
Colonna, Cardinal Odo de, 38, 40-41, 47
Concerning Simony of Hus, 17, 49, 64
Conciliar principle, 60
Constantine, Emperor, 63
Cossa, Cardinal Balthassare, 28
Council of Constance, 3-4, 14, 28, 30, 34, 42-44, 49, 51-52, 55, 60, 62, 68, 70-72, 74-75, 77; Bishop of Constance, 53; Constance, 57, 65, 69
Council of Pisa, 33, 65, 73
Council of Trent, 76
Czech native reform movement, 5, 6, 8, 41-42, 46-47, 78

d'Ailly, Pierre, 14, 30, 70-72
Daughter, The, of Hus, 19
De corpore Christi of Hus, 26, 57
De ecclesia of Hus, 10, 15-16, 49, 62-63, 69
De indulgenciis of Hus, 10, 18
De ecclesia of Páleč, 50
De corpore Christi of Stanislav, 22
De universalibus of Stanislav, 21
De benedicta incarnatione of Wyclif, 16
Decalogus of Wyclif, 16, 37
De corpore Christi of Wyclif, 28
De ecclesia of Wyclif, 14-16
De officio pastoralis of Wyclif, 17
De officio regis by Wyclif, 40
De potestate papae of Wyclif, 15-16
De probationibus propositionum of Wyclif, 37
De Trinitate by Wyclif, 37
Dialogus of Wyclif, 28
Donatism, 31-32, 38, 59

Expositio decalogi, or *Decalogue,* of Hus, 17-18, 36, 49
Exposition of the Faith by Hus, 17-18, 49, 57
Exposition of the Lord's Prayer, by Hus, 49

Fitzralph, Archbishop, 20
Flacius, Matthias, 4
Frederick the Wise, 42

German Reformation, 42, 77
Gerson, Jean, 14
Gratian, 12, 14, 64
Great Schism, 31, 32, 60
Gregory the Great, 12, 63-64, 68
Gregory Nazienzen, 68
Gregory XII, Pope, 33, 61, 66, 72-73
Groote, Gerard, *The Following of Christ,* 13
Grosseteste, 14-15, 20

"Nations" at the University of Prague, 22, 34
Neander, Augustus, 4, 5
Novotný, Václav, 6, 17, 19, 31

Ockham, William of, 14, 20
Odložilík, O., 1

Páleč Stephen, see Stephen Páleč
Peter of Stoupno, 28
Philostratus, 14
Picard Brethren, 4
Postils of Hus, 18, 46, 66
Prague, 18, 29, 36, 39-40, 42, 48
Protiva, John, 31-32

Regulae veteris et novi testamenti of Matthew of Janov, 5, 8
Remanence, doctrine of, 22, 26-28, 31-32, 43, 57-58
Remigius, 64
"Replica . . . contra . . . Ioannem Stokes," by Hus, 42
Robert, Hus's jailor, 57
Roman curia, 26, 28, 40
Ruprecht, Emperor, 33
Rvačka, Mařík, 31

Sedlák, Jan, 15-17, 19
Sermones of Wyclif, 19
Shakespeare, William, 14
Sigismund, Emperor, 41, 53, 69, 71; granted "safe conduct" to Hus, 51-53
Sophia, Queen, 25
Stanislav of Znojmo, 14, 21, 22, 25, 26, 27, 28, 44, 46, 47, 50, 62; his De corpore Christi, 22; De universalibus, 21
Stašek, one of the "martyrs" of 1412, 46
Stephaneschi, Cardinal Peter degli, 48
Stephen of Kolín, 6, 27-28, 43
Stephen Páleč, 22, 27-28, 44, 46-47, 49-51, 58-59, 62, 68-69; his De ecclesia and Antihus, 50, 68; Tractatus gloriosus, 45, 68
Stokes, Dr. John, 42
Sylvester, Pope, 63

Tábor, 48; Taborites, 76
Taylor, Henry O., 13
Thomas Aquinas, 15, 53, 68
Thomas à Kempis, Imitatio Christi, 13
Thomas of Strassbourg, 17
Tiem, Wenclesas, Dean of Passau, 43, 44
Tractatus gloriosus of Páleč, 45, 68
Trialogus of Wyclif, 28

Unity of Brethren, 3, 76; their Confession of Faith of 1535, 3
University of Cambridge, 42
University of Leipzig, 34
University of Prague, 21-22, 28, 33-35, 42-44, 47, 54
Urban VI, Pope, 60
Utraquists, 67

Václav, King, 29, 33-34, 38-39, 41-45, 47, 71

Waldensians, Lombard, 32
Waldhauser, Conrad, 5
William of Pérrault, 14-15, 20
William de St. Amore, 6
Workman, H. B., 14
Wyclif, John, 8-12, 14-23, 29, 31, 42, 53, 55-56, 59-60, 67-68, 76; condemnation and burning of his books, 34-35, 37-38, 53; his forty-five articles, 23, 28, 47-48, 54-70; his writings: De benedicta incarnatione, 16; Decalogus, 16, 37; De corpore Christi, 28; De ecclesia, 14-16; De officio pastoralis, 17; De officio regis, 40; De potestate papae, 15-16; De probationibus propositionum, 37; De Trinitate, 37; Dialogus, 28; Sermones, 19; Trialogus, 28
Wyclifites, Czech, 8-9, 19, 21-22, 33, 37

Zabarella, Cardinal, 40-41, 47, 70
Zbyněk Zajíc of Hasenburg, Archbishop of Prague, 24-31, 33-41, 47, 49, 57, 65-66
Žebrák, Castle of, 45, 47